Building User Research Teams

How to create UX research teams that deliver impactful insights.

Steve Bromley

Copyright © 2020 Steve Bromley
All rights reserved.
ISBN: 9781670056849

Building User Research Teams 1

Part 1 - Build the case for research 5

What does user research do for businesses? 8

Explaining why businesses need user research 13

No compromise research 19

Teaching organisations about research 27

Finding allies 33

A budget for research 37

Setting expectations 42

Part 2 - Building research capability 45

Recruiting participants for research 48

Building a user research lab 55

Documenting the research process 65

Using templates to speed up research 69

Storing team knowledge 83

Storing research files 85

Ethical user research 91

Part 3 - Running good research from the start 95

Starting with research objectives 100

Planning research studies 105

Running the study 116

Efficient analysis 123

Debriefing findings 136

Continual iteration 159

Part 4 - After the beginning 161

Team tasks 163

Generating a demand for research 166

Adding new methods 170

Hiring and developing researchers.. 179

Making research collaborative 184

Building a research repository 207

Part 5 - The end 213

Templates 216

Further reading 217

Acknowledgements 219

About the author.. 221

Building User Research Teams

Building products is hard. Successful products require lots of decisions, both big and small, throughout their development process, ranging from 'what feature should we add' to 'what should the text on this button say'.

There are three aspects that need to be considered when making each of these product decisions. Two of these – 'does this further our company's goals', and 'do we have the technical skills required to build this', are not the subject of this book. However, the third aspect is our concern – 'will people want to use this product and do they understand how to do so'. This is perhaps the most important aspect of the three – without users it's very difficult to have a successful product, whether it is a website, app, game, service or physical object.

This book covers all the tools needed to build a professional user research team who can provide answers to essential product questions - 'what would be useful to build?' and 'are we building this correctly?'

Some of the topics covered include:
- Getting people committed to using information about their users to inform decisions

- Avoiding traps that can limit the impact of research
- Budgeting for user research
- Approaches for participant recruitment
- Building a research lab
- Developing the processes and templates needed to run research quickly and reliably
- Storing research files and findings in a repository
- Planning, running and debriefing high quality studies at scale
- Continual iteration of a team's abilities and operationalising research
- Adding new research methods
- Hiring and developing researchers
- Opening the research process up across an organisation

By the end of this book, a new research team should be equipped to plan and run reliable, robust, and repeatable user research that has a real impact on decision making within the organisation, and avoiding many of the traps that cause people to disregard the findings from research studies as 'just some opinions' or 'not statistically significant'.

Through running high quality user research via an established and empowered team, organisations will be able to make better decisions about the products they come up with, avoid putting development time and marketing money into bad product ideas, and ensure that the products created are understandable and useful for the people who they are made for.

This book is for anyone looking to establish and embed user research within an organisation that is inexperienced when working with researchers. That includes lone researchers looking to maximise the impact of their work, new research managers establishing or formalising user research in a new team, companies looking to hire their first researcher or start to embed user research in how they work, and other UX people looking to improve the quality and influence of research they run.

Part one of the book describes why user research is a sensible business decision, and provides tips to help build consensus within an organisation new to research that starting and appropriately equipping a user research team is in everyone's interest and will make everyone look great at their job.

Part two looks at the logistics required before research can be run, including organising participants, defining how research works, and building the tools that researchers will need. By putting this in place, the team can quickly scale once demand grows without losing quality.

An important aspect of establishing a new team is demonstrating the value of user research through doing excellent work. Part three of this book looks in depth at the research process and covers some ways to develop and share best practice so that any researcher can do great work. Some basic knowledge of how to run a round of research is assumed in this section, however, the end of this book also contains recommendations for great books on the basics, if revision would be helpful!

Broadly speaking, there are two ways a team of researchers can be structured. When making recommendations for how to form a research team, this book makes the assumption that a 'centralised' model is being used, where researchers sit together and run rounds of research for a variety of product teams, rather than an 'embedded' model where they sit and work solely within a single product team. The pros and cons of each approach, and how to move towards an embedded model, is described in part four of this book, alongside some other ways of expanding the capability and performance of the research team over time.

In this book, there are some words used throughout that we should explain beforehand, to avoid confusion.

- **Product** is the thing being made, whether that is a real thing (an airplane) or software (the in-flight entertainment system). It can also describe the whole thing (e.g. "we've made an app that sends you bananas on demand"), and compartmentalised bits of a thing ("we make the software that takes payment for the bananas"). Product managers will explain that the difference between a product and a project is that a product is never complete, and iteratively worked on - which is especially useful for researchers because it creates more opportunities to help make the thing better.
- **Product Team** are the people who make the thing. It is not only the 'product managers', but anyone in the team who is involved in making the product, including designers, developers, quality assurance and user researchers, when they are embedded with the rest of the people making the product.
- **Research Team** are the people who are employed as user researchers. In some organisations they will all sit together; in others, each researcher is situated within a product team. Regardless of the setup, we've assumed that researchers work together on sharing techniques, methods and equipment for running research, and the term 'research team' describes everyone in that group of people.
- **Organisation** is everyone at the place being worked at. That will include a lot of people who don't work on the product being researched, not just those from other products, but also everyone who sits outside of product teams altogether - senior management, HR, finance, the receptionist, etc.

Part 1:
Build the case for research

Building User Research Teams

Nobody starts off caring about user research. In most organisations, the degree that people are interested in user research will start out quite low. Perhaps someone senior at the company has heard everyone else is doing it and have hired their first researcher to help make the best possible use of all the very expensive engineering time. Or perhaps they are looking to professionalise the work that product teams are doing already to understand their users, raising the quality of that work, and ensuring that the information everyone is acting upon is robust and sensible. Whatever the reason for hiring a researcher, one of the first priorities for a new research team is to encourage and grow that bud of interest and give the team the space and support needed to flourish.

"Empathy for our users" and "a customer centric mindset" are lovely sentiments, but don't get much traction in a business context, when all the incentives for decision makers are based around making the maximum amount of money possible for the company. Luckily, user research helps achieve that too.

In this section, we are going to look at several of the essential elements for building support and awareness of the value and practise of user research, framed around achieving business goals, which will help set expectations and remove obstacles for a new research team. This includes:

- Explaining what user researchers do and framing the benefits of running studies to inform business decisions around the factors that are important to the company.
- Avoiding many of the compromises that will severely limit the effectiveness of user researchers.
- Finding allies and building relationships with other teams across the organisation.
- Creating and justifying an appropriate budget to run effective user research.
- Setting expectations for how much research is enough.

By the end of this section, a new research team will have raised awareness over their role and the benefits of incorporating information learned from studying users into the design process and will have gained some tools to get financial and emotional support for their work.

What does user research do for businesses?

Every company makes decisions about what they should build or do. Some companies come up with ideas for new products or services to build and make them happen. Others iterate on an existing product, deciding which features they should add, or what future updates should allow users to do.

Those decisions are informed by a whole variety of sources. Some of those sources are trustworthy, such as using analytic data to draw conclusions about what people are currently doing. Some of those sources are less trustworthy - such as the CEO reading an article about blockchain in an inflight magazine and deciding that it is the future.

The goal of a user research team is to improve the quality of those decisions by providing accurate information about user behaviour to inform and evaluate the product and help everyone do a good job.

However, it is not as easy as 'start running studies and good things will happen'. Many organisations are unaware of the consequences of an inefficient development process and are happy with the status quo. Building the case for how user research can help improve development is essential groundwork required before research can be truly embedded in how things are made and prevents the findings from research studies being dismissed later.

How design happens

To recognise how research can help decision making, it is important to first recognise what the decision-making process currently is. There are a lot of different ways in which the 'design process' has been explained before, and models from GDS's 'Discovery'->'Alpha'->'Beta'->'Live', to the Design

Council's Double Diamond which has the steps 'Discover', 'Define', 'Develop' and 'Deliver'.

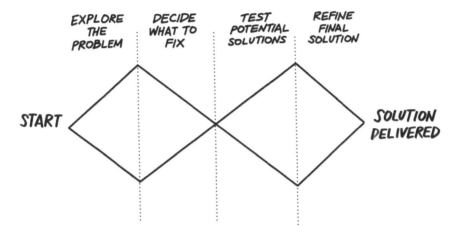

A model for how design solves a problem

At the core of every model of how design works is a process that involves:
- Defining and refining the problem, from a vague idea of what the domain for the problem is, to a clear 'this is what we want to fix' decision.
- Creating and evaluating potential solutions that fix that problem.
- Refining one (or more) solution until it's ready to be put into the world.

These models seem very sensible, and when followed lead to the development of appropriate solutions to problems that exist in the world - design is second only to luck (and possibly marketing) as a factor that will lead to creating something successful. They are applicable to broad topics, such as the creation of an overall product or service, and on a smaller scale for the development of individual features for an existing product.

Even companies that don't explicitly describe their design process probably follow steps very similar to these. A start-up pitching a new app for ordering toast by post should start by exploring whether there is a need for people to get breakfast items delivered to them. Having established that there is a need, they would then test whether 'toast by post' is the right method - perhaps 'grilled pike by bike' would be better for delivering appropriate items in the correct way. Only with the confidence that they are solving a real problem in an effective way would it be sensible to then proceed with making and marketing an app that does this.

This process also crosses sectors, even to industries that would describe their process as creativity - a game designer looking to teach players how the inventory works within their game will follow the same steps of defining what it is they want to teach, trying a method of tutorial that will teach it, and then testing to see if it works as intended.

A 'good' solution will consider multiple dimensions - whether it is possible to create within the time, budgetary, and technical constraints that exist, what the ethical impact of that solution is, whether they have the expertise required to build it. However, one of the most critical things when assessing the suitability of a potential solution is understanding its impact on users - is the solution being proposed dealing with a real problem? And does it work as intended for the people using it?

Because of this, a successful design process is very reliant on understanding the users of a potential product in order to land on creating a good solution. This is where user research fits in.

Where research fits in

Let's return to the model of how design happens:

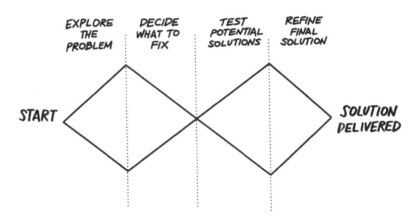

The design process again

And then look at the bits where understanding users better can help.

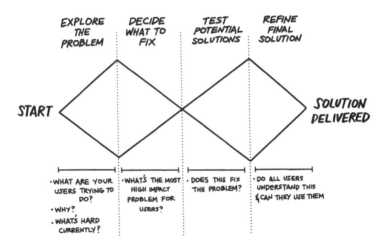

Some research questions that the design process inspires

Early in the development of an idea or feature, understanding the audience it is for will lead to better quality decisions about what to do. By developing a shared understanding about user's goals, their context when acting on those goals and the issues they have currently, smarter decisions can be made about what should be made, and how it should work - for example, if we learned that most people requiring breakfast items in the morning already have cereal in the house, but are frequently out of milk, a new start-up may realise that creating an app to manage a daily milk delivery is more likely to be successful than toast by post.

Later in development, the product team will have come up with some ideas about what to build. Research can help evaluate those ideas before they have been baked in and can no longer be changed, allowing the team to change course if needed and refine the implementation of their idea.

In real life, projects do not follow this process linearly, and there is a lot of movement between these types of research - for example, while evaluative research is looking at the implementation of an idea for a product, new spikes of activity to add features may require additional generative research about the audience and their behaviour to occur. This means that all kinds of research will likely be occurring throughout the development of the process - it is just the frequency of how often that type of research occurs that will change.

The challenge for organisations that don't already have a research team is helping them recognise their existing design process, and how research fits into how decisions get made. We will first look at some of the methods for achieving that and discuss some tools to overcome the barriers to integrating user research in how things get built.

Explaining why businesses need user research

When user research is a new idea, organisations may not understand why they might want it, or what value it brings. Walking teams through the following points, whether via presentations, or drip-fed over time, helps teams recognise the relevance to their role, and advocacy is a core part of building a new research team. Techniques for this are covered later.

The reason all organisations exist is to provide a service or product. Some organisations do this in order to make a profit and allow the founders to buy and sail a yacht to work. Others, like charities or the public sector, do this to make a change in the world (while making enough money, or demonstrating enough value, to continue existing). Regardless of the focus, these organisations all require decisions about 'what to do' and 'how to do it' in order to deliver the product or service.

Those decisions range from big ones, such as "what should the product do?" to small ones such as "what should the label on this button say?" Each of those decisions impact the experience that their users have, and ultimately the success of the product. Although these are design decisions, they are not just made by designers - everyone who makes decisions is impacting the experience being created, from project managers deciding how many developers to allocate to a product, to QA teams deciding which bugs should be resolved prior to launch.

The decisions required go beyond just the digital part of a product. Although Uber is an app on a phone, it makes money by facilitating a service in the real world and understanding and designing every element of that experience is important in order to create a successful product. It is important to recognise that a user's experience with a product will go beyond just a website or an app and include the end to end journey they take when using it.

Each decision made introduces an element of risk, and a poor decision will impact the final product. The consequences of reaching a critical mass of poor decisions are that the product will be poor, greatly increasing the chances of its commercial failure.

Companies who make poor products or services tend not to last long. On the internet the cost to create a rival product are cheaper than ever before - the barrier to entry of many markets is low, and it is simple for competitors to emerge and overtake the company that is first to market. Google wasn't the first search engine; Facebook wasn't the first social network site and Deliveroo wasn't the first company to bring food to people by bike. Making a good quality product is one of the best defences against competitors.

Good decision making is not just important to private companies trying to make a profit. In the public sector, in-house teams are also under pressure to demonstrate the value of their work by making useful things - with the threat of being picked apart, and the work being outsourced to the many big conglomerates that hover around public sector contracts if they fail to deliver. Those conglomerates need to make good decisions also - despite bidding low to get business, failing to deliver a useful product that meets the needs of its users will make it difficult to attract repeat business... hopefully.

So, making good decisions is essential for the success of a business. Making good decisions requires understanding the impact of those decisions. And anticipating the impact requires understanding the people it will impact and measuring whether it is having the anticipated impact. This is where user research brings value to a business.

Explaining how user research reduces financial risk

Making bad decisions is expensive. Many teams spend months or years building something, only to find out no-one wants it after launch. Imagine if there was some way of finding that out before it was built - the team could have built something else instead. Hopefully, something that helps people achieve their goals - a product that people will buy and use.

Similarly, when teams start with an idea for a useful product, they often fall foul of making assumptions about how people will use it. The team making a product are very rarely the same as the people who will be using it - they have different levels of knowledge about the subject matter, they will use it in different contexts, and the product team start by knowing what the product is and how it works, which the users wont. These assumptions, when baked into a product, make it confusing and difficult to use.

User research can solve both problems. By understanding users early in the development of a product, teams can decide whether they are proposing something useful before a single line of code has been written - and it is much cheaper to find that out before spending years of developer time making it.

As development continues, user research can help the team understand if they are on the right track and test the assumptions that they have about their user's understanding and behaviour before launch. This will greatly reduce the time it takes to make a product that works, shortening the development time, and again saving money.

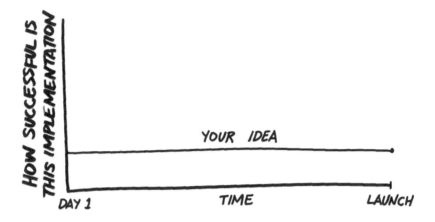

Without outside input until launch, the quality of the product doesn't improve before launch

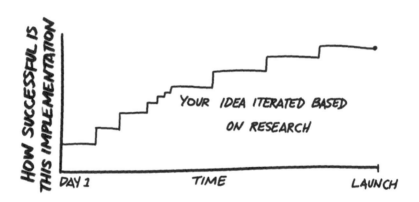

By running user research studies, the quality of the product improves before launch

A common view from people new to user research is that it can be replaced by launching early and iterating. Learning from products post-launch is a valuable source of information to inform iteration. However, it is also expensive when considered long term, because the team is missing out on opportunities to learn and iterate early on, before launch, when less development costs have been incurred.

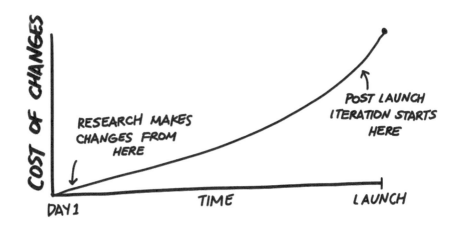

Iteration early in development is a lot cheaper than iteration closer to or after launch

Every organisation is interested in its budget - and promising to reduce development costs while reaching a higher quality product earlier is a powerful message that will help get senior leadership enthusiastic about the potential for user research.

Helping people make good stuff and look good

Making bad product decisions reflects poorly on the organisation. A product that does not solve a problem people have is a product that does not get used, and will eventually be killed off. That is embarrassing and can cause reputational issues that stick around - it has been over 30 years since New Coke launched, replacing original Coke for only 79 days before the decision was backtracked, but people still cite it as a stock example of a bad product.

It is not only bad ideas that impact reputation, but also bad implementation - a product that does the thing it is meant to do but is difficult to use, will also reflect poorly on the company. The video game of the film ET was rushed to meet a Christmas deadline, and was launched with significant usability issues that made it hard to understand what to do, and where to go. It was so poor that it has since been cited as a cause for the crash of the entire video game industry in 1983, and lead to hundreds of thousands of copies of the game being buried in the desert in New Mexico. Bad decisions have big impacts.

Companies don't want to be affiliated with these kinds of mistakes and it reflects well on staff, and the organisation itself, that they make useful products at a high quality.

There's a reason why all the most prominent tech companies have matured and developed UX practises that include researchers working closely with their product teams - it is because they recognise that understanding users helps avoid these kinds of embarrassing mis-steps and helps create great things. "It'll make you look good, and everyone else is doing it" are two powerful arguments that help promote the value of developing a user research functionality within the organisation.

No compromise research

It is relatively easy to get people to agree that user research is a good idea. As covered, it saves money and makes everyone look good - what's not to like? The next challenge is converting that to a commitment of investment in developing their research practise.

Conducting research properly takes money. The budget is covered in more depth later in this section, but some of the costs include:
- Creating an appropriate space to run research
- Sourcing participants
- Incentivising participants to take part
- A researcher's time

This might all sound expensive. But it is cheap compared to the cost of building bad things that no-one wants, and everyone losing their job.

Costs can be scary, and there are several compromises that may be proposed by an organisation interested in dipping its toes into research without spending money. Many of these proposed compromises can undermine the quality of the findings from research studies. Much like with product quality, reaching a critical mass of compromises will cause the research team's studies to be of no value - generating unrepresentative or inconclusive results that do not help the team make better informed decisions. This will impact people's perception of the value of user research and set back any efforts to embed it into how things get built. We want to avoid that.

Some of these proposed compromises can be difficult to navigate, such as...

Why not just use surveys?

Surveys are quick and cheap to run and feel trustworthy because they contain numbers. For this reason, they are often suggested as an alternative to running real user research. However, they are usually a poor method for finding information that is valuable for informing decisions. Surveys are a method for telling us what people *say* they think about things. This is not necessarily the same as what they *actually* think about things. It is definitely not the same as what people will do.

In 2015 Britain had a general election. Polls for months in advance had predicted a hung parliament between the Conservative and Labour parties - consequently, parties starting promising things they had no intention of doing, in the knowledge that they could ditch the promises later when forming a coalition government. One of the things Britain's Conservative party promised was a referendum on Britain's membership of the European Union.

When the votes were counted, the country woke up to a decisive Conservative victory. This surprise occurred because people had been too embarrassed to say they intended to vote for the Conservative party when polled but had voted for them in the privacy of the voting booth. Because of their surprise victory the Conservative Party had to follow through on its commitment to a vote on leaving the EU. Which pollsters predicted incorrectly again, with a huge impact on the future of the UK. 'Shy' Conservative voters filling out surveys untruthfully leading to inaccurate conclusions had happened in exactly the same way in 1992, and yet pollsters still hadn't learned that survey responses are a poor measure of people's behaviour. And behaviour is what is important to understand when making successful product decisions.

As we will cover later, the first step of any study is to uncover "what does the team need to know next?" The objectives of the study will inform the method - whether interviews, usability tests, observation, or surveys will be the appropriate method of answering the study's objective.

Most questions the team will want to know will be based around what people are actually going to do. "Do people really have the problem in their life that this app intends to solve?", "Will they understand what my app does?"," Do people know what this button does?" are all sensible questions that can inform the design of a thing. "What do people say they want?" gives answers that don't match people's real behaviour and is very risky to use to inform the design of something.

Surveys are also limited by the imagination of the person writing the survey. Without qualitative research, it's difficult to anticipate which predetermined options would be appropriate to include in a survey. After results are returned, again without the qualitative research explaining why those opinions or behaviours exist, the utility of the results is limited.

Because surveys do not give information relevant to most of the thing's product teams need to know, they are not very useful, and using them instead of an appropriate research method will impact the product teams team's perceptions about how useful user research is. Despite being cheaper to run than real qualitative research, the harm of doing bad work, especially while the research team is relatively new, makes this method one to be very cautious of.

How about remote unmoderated research tools?

There are tools, like usertesting.com which allow teams to put their software in-front of users with little effort. By sending a website URL to their panel of users, they send back videos of their participants using the website and commenting on their experience. This can be popular because it is quick (multiple sessions can run simultaneously without a moderator present) and cheap (participants aren't paid a huge amount to take part). Because of this, it is often considered an appropriate tool by companies looking to start doing user research.

However, like surveys, on closer inspection, this method is not as useful as it might seem. Because their participants are all people who test multiple websites regularly, they become increasingly unlike other users. This impacts their behaviour while using websites and makes it dangerous to draw conclusions from their behaviour about what other users would understand or do. This is a sampling bias - creating a difference between 'real' users, and the users being studied.

Additionally, because the sessions are unmoderated (no researcher is with them while they are using the software), there is little ability to ask questions. If when watching the session videos an interesting behaviour occurs, there is no ability to probe deeper and understand why. In moderated sessions, a moderator would be able to identify these behaviours and ask questions then and there to understand why.

This does not mean that remote unmoderated research is entirely pointless. As with all studies, the team should start by deciding what they want to learn. If what they want to learn can be answered by an unrepresentative group of professional testers, then this is an appropriate method - and a fast and cheap one too. However, for more nuanced questions, like "what are the problems *our* users have?", using an inappropriate method won't get useful results.

As a research team's influence grows, the wider organisation should quickly see the limits of this type of method and the need for studies that allow them greater control over who is recruited, and greater ability to probe deeper into the behaviours that occur.

We have analytics already

Analytics are great, and an important part of building a complete understanding of the behaviour of users. However, they can only provide a partial understanding of users, and for some contexts.

Analytics can show some parts of what people are doing, but not why that behaviour is occurring. Understanding why the behaviour occurs is essential when making appropriate decisions about what to change. It is also important to be aware that analytics are only seeing a slice of a user's experience, and their whole end-to-end journey also included a lot of things that happened off the website, or in the real world. Building a strategy that combines insight from analytics with understanding of motivations from qualitative studies is a powerful combination to inform decision making.

Additionally, analytics can only show behaviour on launched products. As covered previously, it is cheaper and easier to make changes earlier in the development process. By relying exclusively on analytics, it delays when issues are being discovered, with financial impact. When establishing a new user research team, ensuring that they have a variety of methods available to them is key to being able to provide high quality answers to team's questions.

Can you use people we know/our friends/favourite customers as participants?

Recruitment costs money. It takes a lot of time to find appropriate participants - later in the book we cover appropriate strategies for doing that - and time is money. Also, money is money, and paying participants is important to ensure that they turn up for research, and the study can run in an appropriate time frame.

Because of this, there is the temptation to skip all the hassle, and use people who are convenient. That can be colleagues, friends, or some customers or existing users who are especially friendly.

There is a risk when using these people, and it requires care to avoid them impacting your study. As with the remote unmoderated tools, it is unlikely that these people will be the same as the people who your product is aimed at

- They may know too much or too little about the subject you're looking at to represent the 'real' users accurately
- They know you, and want to be nice to you

These factors impact their knowledge, motivation and behaviour, which means that for many studies they won't be appropriate users. It does not mean that these people are never useful, but for research questions that require learning about your real audience, or understanding your real users' behaviour with your product, finding real users is essential to getting useful results.

We've added "UX" to the front of the existing job titles and popped it in our job descriptions.

Great! But unless the organisation is planning and running studies, and using the results to inform design decisions, then it is still doing the same thing it always has. Running user research studies requires time and attention and is difficult to combine with doing other jobs at the same time - it is probably better to do one job well than two poorly.

There is nothing wrong with being a 'UX developer' or a 'UX/UI person'. But without being given the appropriate time and support to run studies and understand users, the 'U' is lacking.

Isn't this what our market research team do already?

Market research is often an established discipline in many organisations by the time a user research team joins, running focus groups and surveys to help understand people's opinions about the things being built. Because some of their tools are the same as user researchers, there will be some confusion about the roles and responsibilities of each. Some people may assume that this correlates with the method (market research does quantitative work, user research does qualitative), but that is not particularly true - the method is defined by the research objective, and a mature user research team should be confident at running quantitative studies when required.

The goal of a market research team is different to what a user research team is trying to achieve. A user research team will be trying to learn about the audience so that the product can be crafted in an appropriate way. A market research team will be attempting to learn about the audience so that the product can be described in a way that sounds appealing. Although a market research team also runs studies, their research objectives and standards are often very different - using methods like focus groups that wouldn't be appropriate for user researchers for learning deep information about people's motivations, or creating personas focused around demographics or attitudes rather than behavioural insights.

Due to the crossover in terminology, methods, and product teams being worked with, there is a risk that the two roles get conflated. This is not a good thing for a new user research team - because of their different goals and standards, it will make it harder for people to understand what a user research team does, how the findings are directly applicable to the questions product teams have, and the standard of work that they will be producing. When the suggestion is raised that the user research team should be linked to the market research team, being polite but clear that the roles are distinct is important to avoid issues later.

Let's just launch it and see how it does

Organisations who do not have user research teams often say that it does not matter because they will learn after they launch and cite iteration as an alternative to understanding users. Although it is definitely true that they will learn after launch if the product is useful for its users, and if users understand how to use it, it is a very expensive way of learning and requires throwing away a lot of work when changes inevitably need to be made. Instead, user research offers a variety of methods to discover whether the concept of the product is useful, and if the implementation is going to be successful before launch, which is much cheaper, and quicker, than waiting until after launch. Most organisations would love to find cheaper and easier ways of reaching their goals - and user research offers exactly that!

To incorporate information learned from research studies into decision making can be considered quite radical at some organisations, particularly to those with a history of deferring to client wishes or listening to the highest paid person in the room. A lot of hard work is needed to bring around change in how people work.

If an organisation understands and accepts why the compromises listed above are no substitute for running real research studies, it is an early indication that there is a real desire for user research within the organisation and is an encouraging sign. However, it is not always the case from the start, which is why education is another essential strand for establishing a new research team.

Teaching organisations about research

Bringing around real change in how product teams work is hard. Everyone is fine with 'being informed by the insights from research studies' in theory, up until the point it contradicts what they want to do. When conflict does occur, there is often a reluctance to change direction or revisit decisions that had previously been made.

One of the reasons for this is incentives. The ethos behind user centred design is to build useful and usable things for the people who use it, but many organisations are set up to incentivise things other than 'make something useful and usable for people'. Internal politics and large backlogs can often reward the individuals in charge based on code deployed, hitting deadlines, showing 'progress', and launching on time. When a research study then turns up and says "actually, this thing isn't really working in the way you think it is", if the incentive for 'making useful things' is lacking, it is difficult to make people care about building good things, and the study is ignored.

If people do not have a reason to care about building good things, then user research will fail to have an impact when conflict occurs and running studies will be pointless. Because of poor incentivisation, there can be hostility towards user research because it will contradict how people work. To combat this, advocacy - explaining what user research is and how it will help everyone look good - is just as important as doing good work for building up people's willingness and support for making useful things.

In most companies, driving the growth of the business is considered the most important factor to continued success, and all the internal incentives are set up to encourage this. Consequently, sentiments about building empathy with users does not build much traction, because this is considered secondary to growth. In all the education work a new research team does, ensuring that the business value of running research studies and incorporating the findings into decision making is emphasised is important. This means that explaining how user research helps deliver high quality products for cheaper, should be one of the main messages, regardless of whether that is each researcher's motivation for doing their job.

Find out what's happened before

The first step is to understand what has happened previously, and what people already know about research. It is likely that people will have been exposed to aspects of user research before, whether from previous jobs, previous colleagues or personal interest. It is important to not assume or imply that a new research team are bringing enlightenment to the ignorant masses - no-one likes arrogance! However, it is also necessary to identify and challenge misconceptions that people have about research.

To achieve this, schedule individual 1:1 meetings with people from different backgrounds in the organisation - these should be the first research interviews that the team does. Like any research interview, they will mainly be about listening - not telling.

The research objectives from these interviews are to:
- Learn what their current level of understanding about user research is
- Identify what motivates the person you are interviewing and what their priorities are - what are the incentives that influence their behaviour
- Understand what has happened before regarding user research at this company
- Find allies who are enthusiastic about the potential for research
- Find out who makes the decisions that impact how products get built

By running these interviews with people from across the organisation, a lot of raw data will be captured about the potential for research. Analysing this data (techniques for analysis are described later in the book) will help identify how to position explaining research appropriately so that it seems relevant and useful to the organisation.

Education

Once the current level of understanding and interest in research is understood, it is time to start changing it. In order to respect user research and apply it appropriately, it's important that everyone understands the basics of what user research is. Some steps for using collaborative research techniques to build the product team's maturity are explored in more depth in part four of this book, but for a new team a proactive programme of education about user research is essential.

The goal here is to talk about user research. A lot. There will be a saturation point where everyone is bored of hearing about user research - your goal is to ensure when they reach this saturation point it is because they have understood the points being made and have heard you explain it all before. *"I can't believe that she is telling us again why behaviour seen in just one person is as valid for decision making as behaviour seen in five people"* would be a great place to get too.

There are numerous methods that can be used to ~~band on about~~ educate people about user research and using all of them in combination will help achieve a momentum behind research awareness that is needed to change the trajectory of organisations with low research maturity. These include:
- Creating and displaying posters around the building. Some of the topics that can be covered on the posters include socialising research principles (the focus on behaviour over opinions, putting

assumptions in front of users early, why accessibility is important, exposing team members to user research sessions directly, etc...), the benefits of running research (it helps teams make better decisions earlier), and sharing successful examples of where research has made a difference to a product, including teasers of interesting findings that will inspire people to seek out the study to learn more.
- Regular drop-ins, on a weekly or monthly basis which give co-workers the opportunity to come and ask questions about research in a safe setting. This involves booking a meeting room, sitting in it for an hour to be approachable, and advertising the opportunity to drop-in via digital methods (slack channels, emails, company newsletters), and non-digital (make a sign for the door, and a poster to advertise the drop-in). For the drop-in, prepare some topics to talk about if people attend because they are interested in research, but have no specific questions - such as the basics of what user research is, some of the methods used, and why it is useful to do - focused around the promise of helping staff to make good decisions in their roles.
- Lunch and learns, going in-depth on some research topics to demystify them, such as 'what is the point of user research?', or 'what do the findings of a research study look like?' Providing food can be a good return on investment if it leads to an audience of people ready to be convinced about the benefits of user research. Even when food is not provided, a talk about user research may be a welcome distraction for people bored of eating at their desk. This can be a great thing to invite guest speakers, such as other members of the research community, in to talk at.
- Using the company's social media such as twitter or a blog to raise awareness that research is happening. In many organisations, even a public facing blog's main audience are people who work inside the company, so it can be a great avenue for teaching colleagues about

the theory behind research, and share how other teams are successfully applying it, in order to create a fear of missing out.
- Taking advantage of every existing opportunity to talk to your colleagues - stand-ups, away-days, show and tells, and more. Any event could be an opportunity to remind people about the work and benefits of engaging with the new user research team.

In addition to explaining what user research is using these channels, it will also be useful to help dispel some myths. Some of these will be addressed by the 'no compromise' talking points mentioned earlier. Other common ones include:

- 'User research makes things take longer'. As covered previously, although research activities take time, they reduce the time it takes to discover and create the 'right' product and so reduce overall development time and costs. Some examples showing the increased cost and time needed for making changes near the end of development, compared to making better decisions earlier, will be helpful for demonstrating the value user research can bring to product decisions.
- 'User research is just asking people what they want'. The education sessions can explain that user research is focused on people's behaviour, and the value that understanding behaviour can bring to informing and evaluating product development. Describe that researchers understand the difference between people's behaviour, and their opinions. Explain that because people's opinions will be heavily influenced by the context in which they have been asked, they are dangerous to generalise from low sample sizes and generate poor quality data to inform decision making. Explaining these challenges and reinforcing how the risks are accounted for in the

research practice will be a valuable to build trust in a new user research team.
- 'Anyone can do user research'. While technically true, it is also true that anyone can put up a shelf, but DIYers should probably not be building a house. Making a judgement on how business critical the study is, and what the impact of the results being wrong would be is important when judging to what extent it's ok for non-professionals to run the study. Using education opportunities inside the organisation to explain the problems that running user research, which is neither repeatable, robust or relevant, can cause is useful to help teams understand when they should be running their own research. Sometimes it is unavoidable, and part four of this book discusses some ways to help manage integrating the work of non-researchers with a dedicated user research team.

Another important tool is to build allies across the disciplines, developing close relationships with colleagues to help them realise the benefits of building an in-house research capacity. Let's look at some specifics on how to do that.

Finding allies

Researchers are not alone in their desire to build good things for people. It turns out, most of our colleagues are also trying to do a good job and have the same desire to make decisions that will impact positively on our users, even when working in systems that do not incentivise that behaviour.

Many of the benefits of running user research throughout the development of products applies equally to all disciplines - everyone gets to look cool because they have made something good. However, there are some specific groups who make particularly good allies to have, and some approaches that may particularly resonate for explaining the benefits of research to them. These include:

Making friends with designers

Designers will be your best friends! Their role is to decide how things should work, and 'render their intent' by describing and showing how a product will work to others with enough clarity that it can be built. In larger organisations, the role is often split. 'UX' designers describing how things should work, 'UI' designers describing how it should look and 'content' designers decide which words would be appropriate to use to convey the intended meaning. Every decision that gets made in a project changes how it will work and what the final thing is, but designers are those that are tasked with understanding and directing that mass of activity into a coherent whole.

To do their role well, they need to understand what the challenge the team is being set to achieve is and be able to measure whether they are achieving it. Research can provide a lot of relevant information, not only to help inspire good solutions, which will make them look smart, but also to check that the solutions are working as intended. Because of this, the benefits for designers to work closely with researchers are obvious - they are already conscious of the impact of their decisions on users and so primed for applying the findings from studies. Working closely with an established design team can make getting traction much easier for a new research team.

Making friends with analytic folks

Many organisations have existing analytic functions, using tools such as Google Analytics to look at people's current behaviour. This is hugely valuable information for decision making, and the cross-over with the work a new user research team would do is huge - both teams plan and run studies to explore hypotheses and inform decision making.

Therefore, working very closely with any existing analytics teams is extremely important. They can help find how representative behaviour uncovered in qualitative studies is, allowing the team to draw more holistic conclusions. The relationship can also work the other way, where behaviour observed in analytics will benefit from additional information learned from other studies to explain why that behaviour occurs. Combining these methods can strengthen and increase the utility of the conclusions from both teams. Because of this, it can be valuable to regularly check in about research studies and help identify areas of cross-over.

As the research practise matures, recognising that both the analytics and research teams are taking questions from product teams, deciding the appropriate method, running studies and drawing conclusions can lead to combining the functions, having a shared method of ingesting research questions to take advantage of the specialisms, processes and tools of both teams.

Making friends with developers

A naive understanding of the role of developers is that they make the things designers design. However, this is an incomplete view - developers have a much deeper understanding of the constraints of the medium than most of the rest of the team, and so their input is essential throughout the design process.

Integrating user research throughout the development process promises to help teams get to the 'correct' solution faster. For developers, this means clearer descriptions of what should be built and less throwing away previous work. This should be popular because no-one likes to see their work wasted.

It also gives developers, alongside the whole team, the opportunity to see the impact of their work on real users early, which can be encouraging, and helps people feel greater pride and ownership over the work they are doing.

Making friends with product managers

Product managers balance making strategic decisions about what products should do, with more granular decisions about prioritisation and what teams should focus on next. User research makes their jobs a lot easier. Early on in a product's development, research about the intended users to understand their context of use, goals, current approaches, and the issues they encounter will give rich information about what a successful product might be for them. Similar studies will be run as parts of a product are launched, allowing product managers to continually refine their vision for the future of the product.

Similarly, the evaluative role of usability testing during development will help refine and nuance decisions about what the team should be focusing on by uncovering relevant evidence to inform and justify their decisions. Ultimately, running research throughout the development of the product will lead to a better-quality product - reflecting well on the product manager. User researchers should be very popular with their product managers!

Making friends with everyone

Of course, people are more than their job titles, and pigeon-holing people into certain motivations can be reductive, because people have complex goals and responsibilities. Being open about user research, sharing opportunities to understand the discipline, and learning about the product's users should be an attractive offer to anyone in the organisation - some further techniques for doing this are covered later in the book.

If that fails, bake a cake.

A budget for research

Having convinced everyone that research will make their lives easier and lead to building cool things, the next question that will come up is 'how much will it cost?' Running proper user research is not cheap - although it is cheaper than building software no-one will use, or spending months of developer time on work that will get thrown away.

Some of the major costs that will be incurred are:
- Salary costs for a researcher
- The costs to equip a user research lab
- The software needed to run research studies
- The costs to find and secure participants for research

This means it is necessary to work out how much budget will be required and convince someone to fund it.

Why is an appropriate budget important?

Getting a commitment to an appropriate research budget might be hard. Although compromises are possible, it is important to recognise what those impacts of those compromises are and ensure the budget holder is making a conscious decision that this within the best interests of the organisation.

Some of the alternatives to hiring a professional user researcher include:
- Hiring a contract user researcher on a per project basis
- Commissioning an outside agency to run research
- Using someone who is not a professional user researcher to run studies

All of these are options to consider. However, the contract and agency researchers are often vastly more expensive than the costs of hiring a permanent member of staff. For example, in London currently, it is about the same annual cost to hire a permanent user researcher for a year as it is to get 100 days of contractor time. Or 50 days of a researcher supplied by an agency. When combined with an appreciation of the benefits of retaining the knowledge about users in-house, going for permanent staff members becomes an attractive option to take.

The alternative of using a non-researcher to run a study may seem cheaper in the short term, but it is likely that they will struggle to deliver reliable and useful results, either resulting in a rejection of user research within the organisation or, perhaps more damaging, a bad product based on poorly informed decisions. If a company is serious about using research to inform decision making, they will want to be confident that the information they are gathering is robust and reliable.

The equipment for running research is one of the areas where cutting back is possible. The risk of doing so is that it increases the technical overhead the researcher has to manage when running studies and increases the possibility of sessions failing. The second part of this book describes some potential setups for a variety of budgets that help reduce the risk of failure.

Sourcing and paying participants are the last areas in which cutting back introduces risks. Part two of this book also goes into more detail about the approaches that can be used to source participants, but in brief, the trade-off is time. Spending more money saves more time for researchers, increasing the velocity of testing and allowing researchers to focus on running studies. For many organisations this is worth doing because researchers time costs more than using other recruitment methods.

Much riskier is cutting back on incentivising participants. How people are rewarded for taking part in studies will have a big impact on the quality and type of people that take part, and there is massive risk of sampling bias. If 'swag' from the company is used as payment, only people who value the company will take part - compromising many of the findings about their behaviour or opinions. Paying participants with money (or generic gift vouchers) is a motivator for most people and will reduce the opportunity of sampling bias - creating better quality conclusions and helping everyone make better product decisions.

Ultimately, spending an appropriate amount of money on creating user research capability will help reduce the risk that it will fail. There are many organisations happy to pay lip service to user research, but who are not prepared to have their preconceptions or plans challenged by the results of research studies. Failing to support the user research team with appropriate funding is a signifier for a lack of commitment from the organisation and indicates that they are not that into evidence-based decision making and may ignore inconvenient findings later on. Research studies may be possible to run with no budget but can be compromised. Because of this, it is important to push for enough budget to run research of an appropriate quality (or get out early!).

How much does user research cost?

The figures for this section are based on the UK. The largest tech hub in the UK is London, which is an expensive city. But most tech hubs are in expensive cities - so it may still be relevant outside of the UK.

Researcher salary
According to Zebra People's salary survey, a mid-range user researcher can expect to earn between £30,000 and £55,000, depending on the sector in which they work (working at an agency being the most lucrative).

As mentioned, an alternative to hiring a dedicated researcher could be hiring a research contractor. The same salary survey gave the average daily rate for a mid-range researcher to be between £300 and £425 a day. Calculated over 253 workdays, that contractor cost could therefore be between £75,000 and £110,000 a year.

Lab costs
As covered in part two, user research labs that cost anywhere between £50 and £500,000 are possible. However, a budget of £5,000-£10,000 should be enough to build a reliable setup and get started running research using the tools described later.

Alternatively, it is also possible to hire external labs, useful for teams who do not have a dedicated space available for research. The costs for this can often range from £500 - £1000 a day. Running a test per week could cost between £25,000 and £50,000 a year.

Participant recruitment
The costs for the participant recruiter often vary based on the difficulty of sourcing the type of participant required, and what the participant will be required to do. Getting participants who are particularly niche can cost more when bespoke recruitment methods are required to find them. Getting participants who are particularly wealthy can cost more, because the amount of money offered for their participation will mean less to them and it will take more to convince them to take part. Also, asking for more time from any user will cost more; for example, asking them to commit to a diary study over a number of weeks.

For a user from an audience that is not hard to find or incentivise, the cost of recruiting per individual could be £50-£100. An appropriate amount of compensation for the same type of user could also be £50-£100 for an hour.

A team of two researchers could potentially run a study every 2-3 weeks with the schedule described later. Assuming each study sees eight people, every two weeks, the recruitment costs could therefore be something like £31,200 a year *(£150 recruitment including incentive x 8 participants a week x 26 weeks)*. This cost will increase as the velocity at which research occurs increases.

Setting expectations

It's hard for anyone to do a good job if it is unclear what a good job looks like. It is the same for organisations that are new to research - they are unaware what research is appropriate or expected, which is understandable when they have not done it before. The solution is to set expectations of what research is appropriate and give clear standards for what a good project would look like. This has been done to great success at places like the Government Digital Service (GDS) in the UK, where each of their projects must undergo a formal assessment before going live to ensure that appropriate research has been done.

An approach for this could be creating and socialising some principles for 'what good user research looks like', using the education techniques discussed earlier such as posters, presentations and blog posts. This can be combined with assessments of projects, and rewards for teams that do well. With enough support at a senior level, it can also be combined with consequences for the teams that fail - for example, the assessments at GDS had the ability to stop projects from launching that failed to demonstrate appropriate research had occurred and acted upon.

Some of the principles could include:
- Understand who your users are, and their context
- Explore to find the right solution
- Check your solution works as intended
- Make changes based on what's learned from research

And the evidence that could be reviewed in an assessment includes:
- Can the team provide evidence they have understood who their users are, based on reliable information? This could include research findings about the intended users, such as understanding their

context, current processes and issues, and showing how these findings have been communicated to the team.
- Can the team provide evidence that the solution they have done is appropriate for the users they have identified? This could include running usability testing on prototypes and early builds of the software.
- Can the team provide evidence that they have made changes as a result of what they've learned from users? This could include demonstrating how iterations of prototypes have addressed the issues discovered in usability testing.

Implementing an assessment process is not easy, and successfully doing so requires a huge amount of support from the organisation. There are some risks when it is not provided with appropriate support - most pertinent is if there are no consequences for failing to meet the required standard. Without enough buy-in from people at the most senior level for meeting user research standards, the incentivisation for most teams encourages them to pick "ship a bad thing now" rather than "wait to ship a good thing", making the process of assessing them pointless. Part of GDS's success with assessments was to give assessors control over the project's budget and allowing them to withhold budget as a consequence of failing an assessment. That degree of commitment to quality over delivery is hard to get buy-in for, hence requiring support at the top levels. Without this support, the only consequence of failing an assessment is embarrassment.

Another risk is that by running assessments just before launch, it can often be too late to address issues. For example, if 'toast by post' is being rolled out next week, but the team have not run the research to identify whether people need toast through their letterbox, there is no point running a study since the commitment to building it has been made. Replacing one large assessment with regular small ones throughout the development of a product can help ensure that issues are raised at an appropriate time when the team still has time to react.

Despite these challenges, setting expectations about what user research is appropriate will be very important for embedding it in how things get built. Starting small with assessments, iterating and building enthusiasm by celebrating successful projects that are using user research well will be important to helping organisations adopt running studies as standard practise. Demonstrating the value of this will help convince senior leadership to enforce the standards across their projects and implement consequences for failing.

Part 2:

Building research capability

Running a research study is a repeatable process, and every study goes through the same steps of 'kick-off', 'preparation', 'running the study', 'analysing the findings', 'debriefing the findings' and 'tidying up'.

A researcher can muddle through and do all of this on the fly, but a small amount of up-front work to prepare the research team can begin to operationalise studies and embed the spirit of optimising the research team's workflow into the team from the start. This will lead to studies that are much quicker to run, reduce the opportunity for errors to occur that will impact the results of studies, and free up a researcher's attention so that they can focus on planning and moderating great studies, instead of doing paperwork.

A lot of the work that goes into running good research is invisible and goes beyond the researcher's direct interaction with users. Getting that invisible work optimised will make it easier to do a good job and produce reliable results promptly. In this section we look at what needs to be done to enable those research studies to run smoothly, which includes:

- A variety of approaches to finding people to participate in research studies, from pulling people off the street to hiring a dedicated in-house panel manager.
- Building a research lab with the capability to run studies, for a range of budgets, and the implications of each setup.
- Using checklists to recognise, define, and improve how research is run across a whole team.
- Templates that can be prepared in advance that make the admin tasks for a researcher quick and simple.
- Storing the team's growing body of knowledge to share best practice, and where to keep the files that the team generates.
- Ensuring that research is ethical and doesn't break the law!

At the end of this section, a new research team will have all the processes and templates required to start running high quality research sessions that can deliver impactful results efficiently.

Recruiting participants for research

One of the fastest ways for research studies to go wrong is in the recruitment of participants - the subjects of the studies that the research team will run. The goal of a research study is to learn something about user's behaviour or motivations, which becomes very difficult without timely and appropriate access to users. Yet, it is also difficult to identify that recruitment has not gone well until the study is running when it is too late to do something about it.

Because of this, it is very important to ensure that the process that is established for getting hold of participants will deliver the representative participants researchers need. There are three common approaches that teams can take to find participants - ad-hoc, using an external participant recruiter, and hiring someone to recruit full time. Let's look at each in turn.

Ad-hoc participant recruitment

Ad-hoc participant recruitment covers a wide range of methods, from asking colleagues to be research participants, to finding people off the street, or asking favours from existing customers. A typical approach for doing this may involve going somewhere users are, asking for a few minutes of their time to help with research, and rewarding their time with gift vouchers or cash.

This method requires much less preparation than other recruitment methods, because it is ad-hoc - and can be run at any time - whereas more formal recruitment methods can take 2-3 weeks to find and schedule the participants required.

It is also cheaper; the only cost is the incentive given to the participants - and because the commitment from participants is low, the value of the incentives needed can be lower than other methods. As ad-hoc participant recruitment is quick and cheap, it is often considered an appropriate approach by organisations with a low commitment to user research.

However, organisations frequently do not consider the downsides of this method. Because this recruitment method is informal, it is very difficult to get a long-term commitment from the participants - it will be hard to find people who will participate in a session longer than 30 minutes. This puts constraints on the methods that researchers will be able to use for studies, making it difficult to answer many of the more interesting research questions a team might have.

Despite being quick to organise, ad-hoc recruitment can also greatly increase the amount of time the data collection part of the study can take. Unlike other methods, the participants are not scheduled in advance, and so there can be long gaps between finding appropriate people to take part. The informality of this recruitment method greatly increases the potential for dropouts in the session - users failing to turn up, or dropping out unexpectedly. This overhead is a poor use of a researcher's time - their primary skillset is in the collection and analysis of data, not in scheduling and organising participants. It becomes very costly to have all these expensive researchers sitting around doing nothing when participants fail to turn up.

Most importantly, the informality of ad-hoc recruitment greatly compromises your ability to identify and screen participants to make sure they are representative of the product's users. This creates a sampling bias - that the people participating in studies do not match the people the product team needs to learn about, compromising a researcher's ability to draw conclusions about their user's behaviour and opinions. Not only is this an issue with the data itself, but it can also impact the perception of the research findings when shared with others - if people start to question the validity of the findings, trust is broken.

Ad-hoc participant recruitment isn't *never* the right method of finding users, but there are huge risks, and it does not increase the organisation's trust in the findings from research, which will cause the findings to be dismissed - wasting everyone's time. When poor recruitment leads to poor research, it can be more detrimental than doing no research at all.

Using an external participant recruiter

An external participant recruiter is an individual or company that will help find and schedule participants for research studies, for a cost. They often combine an existing database of potential users, with bespoke recruitment activities to help source people who match the needs of a study.

The process for each individual round of research typically involves a briefing with the recruiter to describe the details of the study - the dates, times, and the type of people required (e.g. "people who come to our website currently, at least once a week"). They then perform whatever recruitment activities they feel are required, until they have found enough appropriate participants, which they will then schedule into the times you've agreed.

The benefits of outsourcing participant recruitment for a research team are obvious - the impact on the researcher's time from recruitment is minimal after the briefing, and they are free to focus on the other tasks needed to prepare a study. As specialists, the recruiters can dedicate their attention and time to ensuring quality participants are recruited and chase them to ensure attendance.

Consequently, this method costs more than ad-hoc recruitment, and participant recruiters usually charge a per-participant fee for each person they find. The incentives paid to participants may also be higher than ad-hoc recruitment, because they will have to travel and have planned their day around taking part in the session. However, in return, external participant recruiters will find higher quality and more reliable participants.

There are many user research participant recruitment companies, that can be found by searching on Google. Some questions to consider when deciding which to work with include:
- Do they know enough about my industry that I can trust them to identify appropriate participants?
- Are they prepared to go find appropriate participants if they are not already on their database?
- Do they take responsibility for mis-recruits (participants who weren't appropriate)?
- Are they responsive and do I trust that they will be ready to help if issues occur with participants on the day of the test (e.g. a participant fails to turn up)?
- What steps will they take to refine and iterate the quality of the participants they are providing?

An additional benefit of using an external participant recruiter, is that they can often pay the incentive to the participant directly, rather than requiring the researcher to hand over cash. That can be a benefit for many organisations who may be cautious about storing large amounts of money on site.

Dedicated participant recruiters are extremely helpful for ensuring that research can run reliably and regularly and are an essential part of a mature research process. If there is enough budget to use an external participant recruitment company, procuring one should be one of the first things to do - it is easy to underestimate the amount of bureaucracy getting a new supplier organised can require!

Hiring a dedicated participant recruiter

A dedicated participant recruiter is the same service as the external participant recruiter, but in-house. Hiring someone whose sole role is to find and schedule participants can be very valuable and takes advantage of opportunities that external recruiters cannot.

As someone who sits with the team, their level of understanding about the study and the type of people who will be appropriate participants can be a lot higher - they have the opportunity to be exposed to the research sessions, and retrospectives, making it easier to identify and resolve recruitment issues.

An in-house recruiter will also be able to work across the organisation to find opportunities from existing initiatives - for example, the marketing team might have a customer panel already, or there might be opportunities to use existing resources such as the company website to recruit appropriate participants. Unlike researchers, the recruiter will have the time needed to focus on developing and using these opportunities appropriately, while maintaining the high quality of participants needed to run good research.

Hiring a new participant recruiter when the role has not existed before in the organisation will mean that some time will be needed before they can be fully effective. Although they have the time to schedule participants, they will not have a pre-existing database of people to source from, so will need time to build up that panel of users, leveraging the opportunities that exist inside the company, as well as finding creative ways of maintaining and broadening their panel of participants.

They will also be exposed to a high amount of personal data, and need to carefully ensure they are treating it appropriately, sourcing only people who have consented to being contacted, storing their personal details safely and ensuring that relevant legal and ethical obligations are being met. Complying with regulations like GDPR should not be overly burdensome for research teams who are dealing with personal data ethically already - as we will cover later in the book.

Which is the best approach?

Participant recruitment is not an area to compromise on. If the organisation is serious about wanting to make good products that people want to use, participant recruitment is one of the largest costs that they have to meet to run appropriate user research. As a new research team hoping to establish user-centred decision making into an organisation, fighting for appropriate recruitment is one of the most valuable things to do properly.

Therefore, ad-hoc participant recruitment can ruin research sessions before they get started, and often reflects poorly on the quality and utility of a user research team.

When deciding between internal and external participant recruitment, it comes down to a financial decision - ultimately how many studies the team will be running. A rough calculation is that it becomes worth hiring a dedicated in-house participant recruiter when a team can support running two studies a week, but this can change based on factors such as the cost of external recruiters in your area, and local wages. Two studies a week will require 5-8 researchers to achieve, so running the numbers when a team reaches that size would be sensible.

Estimating recruitment costs

One of the first questions a new research team will be asked is to provide a budget for the year. As a regular cost, working out how much participant recruitment will cost will be the bulk of your team's expenditure.

It is relatively simple to estimate, and example costs are given below which should be changed for your circumstances.

(The recruitment cost per participant + the incentive cost per participant) x the number of participants in an average study x the number of studies that will be run a month x 12 months.

For a small team, this could be:
(£60 + £50) x 6 x 2 x 12

Leading to an annual cost of around £16,000 for recruitment costs - but this will change based on the rate a participant recruiter charges and factors such as the frequency and nature of the studies run.

Building a user research lab

As will be covered later in the book, the decision on the appropriate method to use for a study should be guided by 'what we want to learn from research'. For many research objectives, the appropriate method will involve bringing participants in for studies - this is common for usability testing or other methods where the context of where and how a user uses the software isn't being evaluated.

A research lab is a space dedicated to running these studies - prepared for the efficient running of research studies, with all the equipment needed. By having a dedicated space, the time and effort needed to set up each individual study is reduced, increasing the velocity of the research team, reducing the opportunities for things to go wrong, and allowing the researcher to focus their attention on the design and moderation of their studies.

Some of the things a research lab will be set up to do include:
- Allow participants to use prototype software on paper, mobile devices or computers
- Enable the session's moderator to view what the participant is seeing
- Capture the audio and video from the session to give context to what is seen on screen
- Enable other viewers such as notetakers and the product team to observe what is occurring
- Record what happened in the session for later review

Building a research lab requires permanent use of a room in the organisation's office, in which to put the equipment. The ideal room will be decorated neutrally, with good lighting and the ability to control the temperature of the room. It will also be somewhere easy to access from outside, so that participants will not have to come in via the back, with the rubbish bins.

However, finding rooms in organisations can often be difficult, so compromises will have to be made.

The cost of equipping a research lab can scale, from under £500, to millions of pounds. We will cover three different setups that can be done, suitable for a range of budgets. One approach might be to start with the cheapest option and scale up to the more expensive versions as the demand and interest in user research increases within the organisation.

A budget research lab

It is possible to make a setup that can capture audio and video, and stream it cheaply, based around a single laptop device.

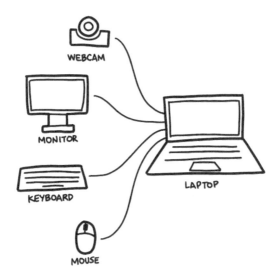

A budget lab setup

The equipment in this setup is:
- A laptop computer with a webcam
- A monitor
- A keyboard
- A mouse
- An external webcam

And some software:
- Obs (Open Broadcast Software)
- Google Hangouts
- Vysor/Apowersoft (if testing on mobile)

In this setup, the laptop is used as both the test device and the hub for recording and sharing. By connecting an external monitor, keyboard and mouse to it, the participant will be able to use it as-if it is a desktop computer. Meanwhile, the laptop's screen will mirror the monitor and allow the moderator in the room to see what happens on the screen.

The software Obs is free and allows a variety of video and audio feeds to be mixed and recorded to the same video file. This allows the moderator to record both what happens on screen, and the webcam capturing the room video and audio into a single video screen, to be analysed later.

Google Hangouts will then allow the Obs window to be streamed to other viewers, such as the note-taker or the product team by setting the laptop as the presenter and sharing the Obs application. This will only work while Obs is not minimised, so drag Obs off-screen during the session so it does not disrupt the participant.

If testing mobile devices, there is software that can mirror what happens on the phone to the laptop, which can then be added to the video captured by Obs. Quicktime on Macs will mirror iOS devices and is free, but PC paid for alternatives do the same - Vysor if testing Android devices, Apowersoft if testing iOS devices. Apowersoft works without a wired connection between the phone and the laptop, which can be particularly helpful.

Combining this mobile feed with a cunning overhead placement of the webcam will capture what the person is pressing on the phone, in addition to what the phone screen is showing, and can be useful for identifying when participants press inactive elements. With slightly more effort mobile 'sleds' that mount the camera can built or purchased which mount the overhead camera to the phone, improving the quality of the video captured from it - one of which we will look at in the mid-range setup.

This setup is very cheap - particularly if the researcher already has a laptop. However, it has some limitations that mean a research team may want to upgrade to a better setup. This setup is heavily reliant on the laptop as both the test device, streaming, and recording device. This may impact the performance of the laptop, and if it breaks, the entire setup is lost - making it hard to resolve issues that might occur during a session.

The streaming of the session is reliant on Google Hangouts, which will be routed through the internet before it reaches the viewers. This puts it at risk of video quality being degraded, or complete failure, based on the speed and quality of the internet connection available. An outage from Google would also prevent the research session being streamed, which would be difficult to anticipate or mitigate.

Picking up good quality audio from a webcam will also be difficult with this setup. The microphones on webcams are often optimised for someone directly in-front of it - in research sessions the participant may move around more than anticipated, and audio will be lost which will be frustrating for viewers and mean notes from the session are lost.

This budget setup is often a good start, for organisations who are at the start of building a research team and need to demonstrate the value of running studies quickly. It is also a setup that could be constructed from equipment that is laying around anyway, useful in organisations where procurement and purchasing can take months. However, once research is occurring regularly, the limitations of this setup will start to cause technical issues, admin overhead, and additional complexity that an efficient team will want to minimise. This is when an organisation might consider investing further in a research setup, an example of which we will cover next.

A mid-range research lab

With a budget between £5,000 and £10,000 options for a much more robust lab setup become available.

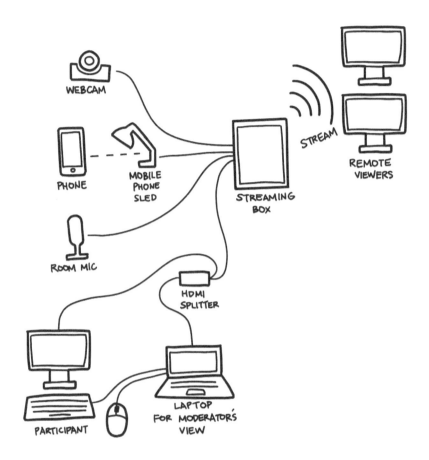

A middling research lab

The equipment for this setup:
- A dedicated streaming/recording device (e.g. the Epiphan Pearl)
- A laptop
- A monitor
- A keyboard and mouse

- An external webcam
- 1-2 dedicated microphones (e.g. the Samsung Go)
- A mobile phone sled (e.g. Mr Tappy)
- A HDMI splitter

This setup replaces using the Obs software with a dedicated hardware streaming box as the centre of the setup. Into this box is plugged the microphone and webcam which will capture what happens in the room. The laptop is still plugged into a monitor, but the HDMI signal is split so that in addition to going into the monitor, it is also captured by the streaming box.

A streaming box, like the Epiphan Pearl, can handle both recording sessions, as well as acting as a web server so that anyone on the same network can stream the session at their desk, or it can be piped through to an observation room. This removes the reliance on a good internet connection for viewing to work.

By decoupling the test device (the laptop) from the recording/streaming setup, it is much easier to recover from things breaking without having to redo the entire setup, and it becomes a more reliable setup for running studies.

This setup also adds one or two dedicated condenser microphones, which can be positioned close to the participant, ensuring that the audio from the session is captured correctly and that details from the session are not missed by viewers.

By using a dedicated mobile testing sled, such as Mr Tappy, the video feed from a phone is much improved. The sled attaches to the phone with magnets, allowing the participant to pick up and move the phone as they normally would while the video feed continues to be captured from the device. The sled can also be used without being attached to a phone to capture overhead shots when appropriate for other studies - for example when running card sorts or looking at physical prototypes.

This lab setup will enable regular lab sessions to be run with minimal technical overhead, allowing researchers to focus on the other aspects of preparing for a study. However, there are always ways to improve…

An expensive research lab

Over time, it will become apparent that some aspects of the lab setup are causing issues or creating duplication of tasks that can be optimised. There are many ways a lab setup can be improved, and almost infinite money could be spent on doing so. Some of the areas a team might consider include:

- Adding sofas and chairs to the room to support a greater variety of seating layouts that can be used for studies.
- Adding mounted overhead cameras to get a wider view of interviews or group discussions; or cover other parts of the room for different types of studies.
- Additional separated places to seat participants so that more than one participant can be seen simultaneously for studies where 1:1 moderation isn't required.
- Automating the recorded video being shared with relevant viewers across the organisation.
- Giving viewers the ability to decide which audio/visual feeds they watch during a session.
- Increasing the streaming capability so sessions can be viewed beyond the local network.
- A tea and coffee machine for participants (or thirsty researchers).

All of these offer the potential to improve the quality of the participant experience, reduce the administrative burden on researchers, and reduce the potential for failure, which will remove distractions during the study and make finding information from users easier. However, one of the most impactful areas to work on is improving the experience for observers.

The observation experience

The reason researchers are paid to run research studies is to inform decisions being made by the organisation, and researchers are rarely the people who have the appropriate authority to make those decisions. This makes communicating what a researcher has learned from their studies the most critical part of their role. A researcher will apply a whole bunch of methods to achieve this, but one of the most powerful is exposing decision makers to participants directly, by streaming the sessions.

In the budget and middling lab setup, a method of streaming the video from sessions was described and asking people to watch at their desks is always an option. However, watching sessions at a desk is not a great experience for the observer - there is a lot of potential for distractions. It is also a very lonely experience, and there are limited opportunities to discuss, reflect upon and improve the viewers understanding of what they have seen.

In part four of this book we talk about some methods to improve collaborative practise with observers, however having a good observation space makes this a lot easier. The observation room is another dedicated room, close to the research lab and could feature:

- A projector broadcasting the video from the research session
- Appropriate speakers so that all the participants can hear the session well
- Whiteboard walls, and plenty of room for collaborative note taking exercises
- A healthy supply of post-its and pens

- Logistical details about the study being run, and the objectives of the study, to set viewers expectations
- Rules for best practise in observing and note-taking prominently displayed
- Refreshments and snacks

By creating a good atmosphere for viewing the research sessions, it will encourage increased attendance, focused attention, and collaboration amongst observers. This will make the researchers task of communicating the findings later much easier, because people will be familiar with what occurred and will find it easier to believe and act upon the conclusions.

Documenting the research process

When first starting in a new organisation, one of the most valuable steps is to create an open and editable checklist called 'how to run a round of research', which can be accessed and edited by the research team. This is a printable one-page document that lists of all the tasks that a researcher should do for each round of research. The intent is that it can be duplicated for every round of research that is run (and 'ticked' as each part is completed).

The start of a research checklist

This list is not only a training tool, there to remind the researcher what they should be doing and minimise errors, but by continually updating the list it is also a useful tool for sharing across user researchers the best practise that has been developed within the organisation when running research. Links from the list can point towards more in depth guidance and templates.

Having a list of steps for each stage of a research project is important for exposing the process and workflow of research - which can then be optimised and inefficiencies removed when looking to operationalise research.

Although a one-page document like this is very helpful for printing, it is not the only way to achieve this. There are a range of digital tools that may be appropriate; for example, a templated Trello board can also be used to track the completion of each task for a round of research.

This list is broken down into the stages of research, which we will go into more depth on later in this book. Those stages are:

Kick Off

The kick-off is the meeting where the product team who are interested in testing agree on the purpose of the study, the appropriate research method to use, and the logistics - when and where the study and debrief will occur.

The items within the kick-off section should include the logistics around that meeting, such as ensuring that the researcher has seen appropriate in-progress work that they can understand what is being evaluated, making sure the goals of the study are captured, and communicating the test dates to everyone relevant.

Prepare the study

This covers the time where the researcher is preparing the materials needed and logistics for the study to occur.

The items in this section should include steps such as scheduling the participants, creating the discussion guide, consent form, note taking templates, designing questionnaires, piloting the study, informing reception to expect the participants, remembering to print things, sending out calendar invites, getting experience with the code, and all of the other things that the researcher will have to do to ensure the study runs smoothly - covered in more depth later in this book.

Running the study

This section covers the time when the study is running. There are usually not too many items on the checklist for the day of the test - everyone will be too busy running the study to review a checklist.

Analysis

The analysis section, when researchers are reviewing the data from the study to find the meaning, is also relatively free of checklist options - everyone's attention is focused on interpreting the findings.

Debriefing & Wrapping up

In contrast, having concluded the study, there are a lot of admin tasks that are important to remember to do, to ensure the results are shared appropriately and best practise captured.

In addition to preparing and running the debrief to the team, the steps in this section can include uploading and sharing videos, storing consent, updating team records on research, providing feedback to the participant recruiter, and running a retrospective on the round of research.

Continuous improvement

As mentioned, making this list is one of the first steps for making research into a regular and repeatable process. However, as the team develops, it will continue to encounter issues that will need additional steps to resolve, inefficiencies that should be removed or identify best practices that should be followed. By regularly reviewing the checklist and updating it, that knowledge can be disseminated throughout the team.

It is important to recognise that a research checklist should not be prescriptive - each individual researcher should be trusted to make the decisions they feel are appropriate in order to achieve the 'true' goal of giving their team appropriate information to make good decisions. When explained appropriately, the checklist should be considered a backbone that can be used to teach and support researchers, but researchers should be encouraged to explore their own ideas about how to run good research, and incorporate any best practise that emerges from that back into the checklist to share it with others. The process for reviewing completed studies and updating the checklist is detailed later in this book.

Using templates to speed up research

Creating a checklist recognises that running a round of research is a repeatable and optimisable process. This also means that the materials a researcher will need for each round will often have a high amount of repetition between them, and can be made into templates, reducing the amount of duplicate work that needs to be done for each round. This can greatly speed up the amount of time it takes to run and debrief a round of research.

The webcomic XKCD neatly summarises the balance between the amount of time that will be saved by making templates and the amount of time it takes to make them - although it assumes that the research team is always operating at peak efficiency. In reality, making and improving the templates can be useful team tasks for when there is down-time in research (more on this in part four). However, for a team of researchers there are also other benefits in addition to time saving - capturing best practice within the template will help the whole team take advantage of the knowledge of others, as well as reducing the opportunity for errors to occur.

The XKCD comic covers when it's sensible to template or automate a task.
XKCD 1205 by Randall Monroe, licensed under CC BY-NC 2.5

We will look at each template in turn, but some parts of a study that can be templated include:
- The kick-off document
- The study plan/discussion guide
- The consent form
- The participant information sheet
- Information for security
- Viewing information for observers
- Note-taking
- Debriefing

The kick-off document

The kick-off document captures all the information that has been agreed at the start of a study. By templating this, we can make sure that all the information a researcher needs to discuss and agree with the product team has been captured, and that the study is in a good place for research to begin. A potential format for this is a document, made using Microsoft Word or Google docs. Longer term, this could also be created as a form - which would enable the information within each section to become structured data that could be used elsewhere; such as in a research repository (covered in part four). For example, by having a field that captures the method used for each study, later on this can be exported to a spreadsheet if the team ever needed to identify every round of research that had used a particular method.

The start of a kick-off document, which can be templated

The document should capture the following information, which can be the headers on the template, with blank space for the details to be added:

- The subject of the study
- The round of research
- The researcher
- The objectives of the study (what do the team want to learn)
- The method that has been agreed to use for this study
- The criteria that is being used to determine appropriate users
- The dates for when the test stimulus must be ready (e.g. the prototype that will be tested)
- The dates for when the study will happen
- The dates for debriefing
- Who the results will be shared with

In part three of this book, we talk through some tips on how to run a successful kick-off meeting. Creating and filling out the template for the meeting can be a useful tool to ensure that the study is understood and agreed by all.

The study guide

The study guide (or discussion guide) is the document that describes what will occur during the session. It has two goals - primarily to guide the moderator during the session, but also it is a communication tool to explain the study to observers and the wider product team.

Because of this second goal, it is important to ensure that it explains the reasons behind the things that the moderator will do in the study. By creating a template, this can be made easier for the researcher to articulate.

The start of a study guide, the outline of which can be templated

The study guide should include a space for the research objectives - for people whom receiving the plan is their first exposure to the study. The template can prompt researchers to copy and paste this from their kick-off document.

A study will usually start with the introduction for the participant from the researcher, and this script can be templated. It can include:
- Explaining what is being consented to in the consent form
- Introducing the moderator, the organisation and the purpose of this study
- Explaining that they aren't being tested, and that they should mention if anything is difficult or confusing
- Explaining that the moderator did not make the thing being tested, and that they should feel safe to give negative feedback

The study guide would then include any pre- and post-interview questions the researcher intends to ask to answer the study's research objectives, as well as the tasks to set the participant. A reminder to start recording the session is also a good idea!

The template can also give a guide for how each task can be captured. A potential format for this is a table, as follows:

Task: <<What is the task that participants will be asked to do?>>		
What we'll ask: <<capture questions to ask during the task>>	**What we'll observe:** <<capture what the researcher will be looking out for>>	**What we will learn:** <<what research objectives does this task address?>>
Post Task Questions: <<What will we ask after this task has been completed?>>		

This templated task table can then be duplicated by the researcher as required.

The consent form

The consent form is the form that the participant will sign to say they consent to taking part in the research. Although some elements of this will be bespoke to each specific study (for example, describing what the purpose of the study is, and what information will be captured), plenty of it will be the same for every study the team runs, so can be templated.

Significant parts of the consent form can be templated

The consent form template should contain the text that explains:
- Who the moderator is and which organisation has commissioned the research
- What steps the researcher is taking to collect and secure personal data
- How long the data from the study will be kept for
- What steps participants can take if they have questions or want to access their data after
- A commitment from the participant to keeping the information within the study secret.
- The purpose of the study and the information that will be captured during the study will be different for each round of research the team runs, but the need to explain them will exist across all studies.

Therefore, the template should have gaps for the researcher to fill this information in.

By ensuring that the template covers all the information needed to be GDPR (and ethically) compliant, the team can greatly reduce the risk of expensive issues resulting from non-compliance!

The participant information sheet

When recruited, whether via an internal or external recruiter, the participant will need some information regarding the study. By creating a template for this, the research team can ensure that they are giving comprehensive information for each session and reduce the opportunities for lost participants.

Common information to give on this template would include:
- The time and date of their session
- The location of the session
- Instructions for what to do when they arrive at the building
- Contact details in case they encounter an issue on the day

If your team works with an external participant recruiter, they will often handle this and so, a template may not be required.

Information for security & reception staff

When the participants turn up, they are going to go to the main entrance of the building hosting the study. To ensure participants have a positive experience before their session, it is advisable to prepare staff within the reception area with appropriate information.

Instructions on how to handle participants when they arrive can be templated

Again, this information can be templated because a lot of it will be the same across multiple studies. It should include:
- The space to put in the date and times of the sessions
- The space to put in the names of the participants so they can verify that they are here for the study.
- What reception or security staff need to know when the participant arrives - for example, a number to call to get hold of the researcher or where to direct them.

By templating this, it will remind the researchers running studies to alert security and help reduce the chance of issues occurring on the test days.

Viewing information

One of the easiest ways to get engagement with the research process from the wider product team is by making the session viewable. We discuss the pros and cons of streaming sessions more in part three of this book, but there are also templates that will be relevant for viewers.

The information that the researcher gives viewers should make it easy for them to understand how to successfully watch user research sessions. The details will depend whether viewing is in-person or via streaming, but in brief it will include:

- A space to put the time/date of the sessions
- A space to put the objectives of the study
- Information on how to view (e.g. where is the observation room, how the video stream can be accessed)
- Information for how to act if they encounter participants in person, to prevent any embarrassing incidents.
- Information on what they should do if they have questions about the research (pre and during the session)

Because a lot of this information is going to be generic across tests, it is also suitable for templating and will help the team share and iterate how they explain research sessions to non-research colleagues.

Debrief template

Sharing research findings with a team can be done in a variety of ways, and the appropriate manner depends on the researcher's relationship with the product team's decision makers.

One of the most common ways of debriefing is a presentation report created in PowerPoint or Google Slides. This format allows the findings to be captured in a way that is both suitable for presenting to teams immediately after the session, but also to be understood by people re-reading the report years later who were not part of the original project. A more advanced format for capturing the research findings for long term analysis would be one that supports extracting the findings as structured data - which we will discuss further in part four.

A report template is likely to comprise of similar sections across studies, and the explanations within it are likely to improve as the team's maturity grows. Because of this, it is one of the most important templates a researcher team can make and maintain.

The first section is likely to be the introduction. This will include the title slide, naming the round of research, a content's slide which can be templated (if the order is often similar), a slide for an exec summary summarising the broad findings from the study on a single page, and slides where the research objectives, method and audience can be explained.

```
┌─────────────────────────────────────────┐
│  EXEC SUMMARY                           │
│  ─────────────                          │
│                                         │
│    THIS ROUND OF RESEARCH LOOKED AT...  │
│                                         │
│    WE LEARNED...                        │
│                                         │
│                                         │
└─────────────────────────────────────────┘
```

```
OBJECTIVES
 • OBJECTIVE 1
 • OBJECTIVE 2


METHOD
 1:1 USABILITY TEST WITH 6 PARTICIPANT.
 PARTICIPANTS WERE RECRUITED BASED
 ON...
```

Many of the slides for debriefing can be templated

The main section of the debrief report will be the findings from the study. This is usually preceded by a collection of explanatory slides which are relevant across multiple studies and can be templated. This includes a slide explaining how the severity of issues has been classified (as described in part 3), a slide with caveats about the method and the reliability of the findings (particularly if the study is also reporting opinion data in addition to usability findings), and then a template guiding researchers on how to explain issues.

A format that works well for reporting usability issues is one slide per issue. It should have prompts to describe what occurred contrary to the design intent, describe the researcher's understanding of the design intent, describe what about the thing being tested caused the user to act in this way, and describe the impact on the user's experience.

```
<<FINDING TOPIC>>
<<FINDING>>
  o CAUSE:
  o IMPACT:
  o DESIGN INTENT:
```

The format for sharing findings can also be templated

Templating a slide that prompts the researcher to describe all these aspects can help encourage researchers to fully describe the issue and ensure the findings can be interpreted by someone new, reading the report at a later date.

After the section for issues, the debrief template can end with common slides that finish a report - for example, an outline for a workshop on resolving the issues or a 'next steps' slide. By preparing a template slide deck that has these sections in already, the workload for researchers is reduced. Because the analysis and debriefing part of a study is a particularly busy time, these templates can have a big impact on reducing the time it takes to complete a round of research. An example of a completed version of this template is included within the debriefing section of part three of this book.

Improving templates

It is important to remind the team that the templates are neither restrictive nor finalised. Not restrictive means that if the researcher believes that they should be doing something different to the templated guidelines, they should be empowered to do so - they know more about the context of their research than the template will! Not finalised means that they should continually be updated - when researchers recognise more tasks that require them to repeatedly perform the same steps each round of research, they should be encouraged to add to the templates or adapt the existing ones to remove duplication in their work. Continually optimising and iterating the research process and templates is of tremendous benefit and is the essence of research-ops.

Although these templates will be unique to each company, adaptable examples of many of these templates are available on the website buildinguserresearchteams.com

Templates are only useful if the team know they exist and can access them as required. Appropriate storage, and supporting information, are important to make the most of the potential of templates, as will be covered next.

Storing team knowledge

As the team grows, 'how to do things' becomes important to document. This reduces the reliability on a single person to know how everything works and ensures that the organisation doesn't have the forbid all the researchers from travelling on the same plane (like the people who know Irn Bru's recipe).

The team knowledge store also serves as an education tool, helping explain to new researchers how to run research and helps create consistency in your processes, allowing them to be optimised, as well as a communication tool for sharing best practice between researchers.

As a list of 'how to do things', the team knowledge can be stored anywhere that supports rich text and hyperlinks. Microsoft's OneNote is particularly good for this as it allows a hierarchy of subjects - for example, an overarching 'tech' section, with subpages for each type of tech system that you want to explain how to use - e.g. 'test phones', 'recording setup', 'test PC'. This hierarchy could also be achieved on a WordPress site (passworded to only allow only researchers to access it, because it may contain device passwords), by making HTML pages for each area. Google Docs can also be used but will not allow the creation of hierarchy within one file, so can be messier.

The checklist, the creation of which was described earlier in this section, is a sensible outline to use for the structure of the team knowledge store. Each item on the checklist could be hyperlinked to a 'more info' page, which gives additional information on how to do that step.

The specifics of how to achieve each step will change based on the context of your organisation, but some good explanations to have include:
- Guidance on what should be discussed in the kick-off meeting

- Links to the templates that have been created for each stage of the study
- Which calendar invites should be sent when running a study, and what the contents of those invites should be
- How to book lab space
- How to recruit participants
- Guidance on how to capture notes from research
- How to use the lab to record and stream sessions
- Guidance for analysing findings from research
- Supporting information for how to debrief findings
- Details for the logistics after a round of research - where to upload videos, store consent forms, store the report, other team records that must be updated.

By linking the guidance for each step to the step in the checklist, the information is available in context when and where a researcher needs it, ensuring it is discoverable. By exposing the guidance to researchers often via the checklist, it will encourage team members to continually iterate and improve that guidance - disseminating knowledge from one researcher across the whole team.

Storing research files

In addition to the researcher-facing 'how to do the job' information, the research team also generates a lot of information from its studies that need to be looked after carefully. This falls into three categories: stuff, deliverables and personally identifiable information. Each of these have different levels of priority, and are for different purposes, and so the way in which they should be stored will be different.

A cloud storage drive, such as Google Drive, or Microsoft's SharePoint, will be behind the storage of each of these categories of files, with some differences based on the needs for each type of file. By using cloud storage all researchers (and the wider organisation) will be able to access the files, regardless of location, which is important when research can be conducted or viewed remotely. Furthermore, some research files can be very large, such as the videos from research sessions, and so the scalability of cloud storage is important to allow it to handle the quantity of studies the team will run.

Remember to ensure that your cloud storage is created at a 'team' level, rather than associated to an individual. In many enterprise environments, using an individual's cloud account rather than a team one can risk all the team's files being lost when that person moves on.

Storing research stuff

When running a study, a lot of files get created. This includes all of the templates that have been adapted and printed out - for example, the kick off document, the study plan, the information that had been prepared for security, and the version of the consent form template that has been adapted for this study. It also includes all the raw notes from the sessions.

Although this information is not immediately useful for anyone after the study has been completed, it is sensible to retain for traceability and repeatability - if a very similar study is run again, it would be useful to be able to adapt the materials prepared last time. Also, should someone question the research conclusions, having access to the raw data that led to those conclusions gives researchers the opportunity to check their findings and provide appropriate supporting evidence.

All this data is suitable for storing on a team cloud drive. Nothing in it should be highly sensitive so, unlike some other data types, this will not necessarily need to be locked down, so only the research team can access it - although it is unlikely any other team will be interested in the unprocessed stuff that gets generated when running a study. The biggest challenge is ensuring there is appropriate structure in the folder so that the information can be found. One way of achieving this is a file structure comprising of the project name, the date of the research (year, month, date so the sort order is correct), which round of research this is and the stage of the study (e.g. preparation, data). This would look like:

//<<project name>>/<<date and round of research>>/<<part of the study>>/file

For example:
New Website/2020 - 01 - Round 1/Preparation/Security Form.doc
Or
Old Website/2016 - 12 - Round 4/Data/Interview Transcript Participant 1.doc

This structure is scalable and allows the navigator to quickly find any specific file from a round of research if they know the project and a rough date. Because there should be no personally identifiable information in these documents, there is no obligation to delete them after a set amount of time.

Storing research deliverables

The deliverables are the outputs of a study that get shared with a wider audience. This often includes a report (such as the template discussed earlier), as well as other files used to support sharing the findings with a wider audience, such as video clips (with personal information obscured).

The goal with these is to make them accessible and discoverable across the organisation, in order to communicate what the research team has found. Although the files are ultimately stored on a cloud storage drive, ensuring that they are discoverable can be difficult to achieve with a shared drive alone - if people do not know it is there, they are unlikely to go looking for it. The files themselves can be kept in the same cloud storage as the other research stuff, using the folder structure described above (i.e. *//<<project name>>/<<date and round of research>>/Deliverables/file*). However, the more interesting challenge is supporting those files with a shopfront that makes it clear what deliverables exist.

There are several potential ways to do this, both virtually and in the real world and a combination of both is important to ensure that everyone in the organisation is reached.
Some of the virtual ways this can be achieved include:
- An internal website that links to the team's recent work
- Posting about it on slack, yammer, and other internal communication tools such as newsletters
- A regularly updated, open spreadsheet that contains key details of every round of research (e.g. what the project was, the research objectives, a direct link to the deliverables)
- Other technical methods of creating an always updated list of research studies are possible using tools like SharePoint and can be automated if the data in the deliverables is structured appropriately.

Combining this with real world methods of communicating that findings exist is important to broaden the audience beyond the most digital of colleagues. This can form part of an advocacy strategy, as discussed in the previous section of this book.

Some ways this can be achieved are:
- Creating posters that can be displayed in the office teasing research findings
- Providing updates on what research has occurred at general staff meetings
- Regular research drop-ins or lunchtime update sessions
- Talking to colleagues

Sticking things on the wall after completing a study can raise awareness of what the research team is doing

Because the reports, videos and other deliverables represent the conclusion of the research team's work it is sensible to retain these files forever.

Storing personally identifiable information

The most important type of files that the research team will be responsible for are those that includes participants personal information. This will include the unedited version of the video recordings for each session, but may also include other files, such as the list of participants or questionnaire responses (if these included personal data such as people's names, contact details, or other information that can be used to identify them). Being responsible for this data introduces legal compliance requirements, and ethical obligations and care needs to be taken with these files.

Being able to trace and find people's personal information if needed is particularly critical. Legislation such as the European General Data Privacy Regulation (GDPR) describes that participants should be able to request to access or amend personal information about them, and so being able to find their files may be necessary. It is also important to ensure that the research team is aware of who has access to this information, and that the consent captured from the participant is appropriate for how their information is shared.

Therefore, although cloud storage is a sensible place to keep this information, tighter access controls will be needed. This can be a locked folder, or an entirely separate drive, depending on the sharing privacy rules available within the tool being used. Within this folder the video files and other personal information can be stored, using the folder structure to help make them traceable - including the date and focus of the study in the folder structure. As will be covered later, consent is granted from users to retain this information for a set period. This means there will be regular tasks to delete old data and storing the files by date will make this easier, which will be required to adhere to data retention standards.

An example structure could be:
//<<year>>/<<month>>/<<project>>/videos/
Which would look like:
2020/01 - January/New Website/videos/Participant 1.mov

This format makes it easy to quickly find and delete all the videos on a month by month basis, at the date agreed when gaining consent. By keeping the participant ID in the filename, it also makes it possible to find all the personal information held on a specific participant - which will be needed if they request a copy of the data that is held about them. Storing a copy of the scanned consent form for each participant in this same section is also sensible, if evidence is required that appropriate consent was gained.

By being aware of what files and data the team is generating when running studies, and storing them in a structured way, it makes meeting the ethical obligations of being a researcher simple.

Ethical user research

Ensuring that studies are ethical is an essential part of creating a functioning research team. Unlike academia there are no review boards who will approve the team's studies before they go live. Despite this, the commitment to running ethical studies is still very important - not only for ensuring that relevant legislation is being adhered to, but also to protect the participants, and to help researchers feel good about working at this organisation.

The legal requirements

The most well discussed regulation in law that impacts research studies is the General Data Protection Regulation (GDPR). Although it is created by the European Union, it also applies to organisations based outside of the EU who work within it, so has had an impact on many businesses worldwide, and aligns with many ethical best practices.

The regulation describes several commitments to how personal data is gathered and stored. Because research studies generate and explore a lot of personal information about our participants, it is extremely relevant to our work, and a research team needs to be prepared for them.

These include:
- The right for participants to be aware of what data is held on them
- The right for participants to access the data held on them
- The right for participants to amend incorrect data held on them
- The right for participants to delete data held on them
- The right for participants to prevent their data behind used

In addition to allowing participants to act on these, there are also some principles to adhere to - like collecting only the data required for a study, only retaining that data while it is needed, and ensuring that data is stored securely.

The consequences for failing to adhere to this regulation can be extremely expensive - with the maximum fine being €20 million, or 4% of a company's annual revenue.

Luckily, all the rules that the regulations require researchers to adhere to also map closely with ethical practice and what a good research team should be doing anyway, so remaining compliant should not be particularly burdensome.

Best practice for ethical research

At the core of ethical research is the idea of informed consent. This assumes the participant should be aware of the details of the study - what they will be doing, why the study is being run, what information is being collected, and what will be done with this data. This is largely handled by the consent form, which explains all the details of the study in plain language that can be understood by the participant. When giving the consent form, it is good practice to explain the contents to the participant also, to be confident that they have understood what they are agreeing too.

Although the consent form is a useful record that consent has been given, it is not the only way in which consent can be captured. For example, when running research remotely, it is not possible to get the participant to fill out a physical form. If written consent can't be organised in advance of the session, in these cases an audio recording of consent being explained, and the participant agreeing that they understand and consent should be sufficient evidence if consent needs to be proven later.

A comprehensive consent form should explain:
- Who the organisation is and who is running the study
- What the purpose of the study is

- What information is being captured in the study (including if the session is being live streamed)
- How that information is being stored, and for how long.
- That the participant can opt out of the study at any point
- How the participant can request, amend or delete the information held on them at a later date.

Giving the participant a copy of the consent form they've signed, or a bespoke information sheet, will allow them to act upon their right to request and amend their information, so is good practice.

It is important to recognise that the consent form is not a legal document. Many teams might want to combine it with a non-disclosure agreement, asking participants to keep secret what they are exposed to in the session. A non-disclosure agreement from a research study is likely unenforceable as a legal document anyhow, but if it is combined with the consent form, extra care should be taken to ensure participants understand which parts of the document the organisation is trying to enforce (e.g. keeping the product secret), and which parts participants have control over (e.g. how their data is used). Keeping consent and non-disclosure separate makes this much simpler.

In addition to handling personal data about users appropriately, a research study also has an ethical responsibility to accurately represent the participants - important to keep in mind when describing their behaviour or issues that occurred during the study. There can be a tendency from people who have not been exposed directly to users to describe their behaviour or thoughts as 'stupid' - perhaps as a coping mechanism to avoid taking responsibility for poor decision making about the product. An ethical researcher will challenge these viewpoints using data from their studies and ensure that the truth of the user's experience is being communicated.

To achieve this, peer reviews from other researchers are very useful - asking other research colleagues to review the study plan, or the findings before they are shared, and challenge that the approach and conclusions are valid. This can be a great tool to build a team understanding of what ethical research is, and how to achieve it.

Part 3:

Running good research from the start

Building User Research Teams

Running the first few studies is the most fragile time for a new research team, which is why it is very important that they go well and show the value of user research early. The organisation has demonstrated enough curiosity to give it a go, but people's perceptions are still fluid - and doing poor quality work will lead to colleagues deciding that research is too abstract, vague or irrelevant to be useful to them. Bad research will lead to study findings being disregarded, the idea of research being dismissed, poor decisions being made, and everyone losing their jobs.

Establishing how the research team works is crucial to being able to do good work, which is why it is important to describe and share the process for running a round of research. As covered previously, when creating the checklist, running a study is the execution of a semi-structured process, which looks like this:

```
CHECKLIST
PRE KICK OFF
☐ REVIEW PROTOTYPE
☐ GET OBJECTIVES
☐ BOOK KICK-OFF
☐ ─────
☐ ─────
KICK OFF
☐ CONFIRM OBJECTIVES
☐ AGREE METHOD
☐ AGREE DATES
☐ ─────
☐ ─────
PREP
☐ PUT REQUEST TO RECRUITER
☐ CREATE STUDY PLAN
☐ BOOK LAB
☐ ─────
```

A research checklist helps give some structure to how studies run

As with the checklist in part two, the stages of running a round of research are:

- A kick-off, which gets agreement on the details of what will be learned from a study, and how it will be approached.
- The preparation stage, where all the pre-work required to ensure a successful study occurs is done.
- The study itself, including moderation and note-taking.
- Analysis, where the raw data from the study is processed and turned into useful information.
- Debriefing, where the findings from the research study are communicated appropriately to people who need to know.

- Reflection, looking at how that study went and identifying opportunities to optimise.

For many studies, the end to end process of running a round of research can take between two and three weeks, although this depends on the method used for the study, and the approach taken for recruitment. There is also the potential to overlap multiple studies - although each individual study may take three weeks, by kicking off a study before the previous one is wrapped up, a round of research can be occurring every two weeks. Later in this section we will look at the specifics for timing a round of research.

After completing a round of research, the process then repeats again. By following a regular semi-structured format, researchers can set expectations and communicate the process to colleagues who are not researchers. Product managers, designers and other colleagues can use the process to learn how a study works, and where they can be involved. This reduces the opportunities for upset people - not only researchers getting input too late to be able to do anything about it, but also product teams who miss the opportunity to influence the goals of a study.

By recognising and describing the research process, each part of it can be compartmentalised, and then optimised in turn. This compartmentalisation, reflection, and improvement has been described recently as 'research-ops'— the practise of looking at the parts of a research study works and finding ways to improve them, including making specialist roles to focus on some parts of the process. A practical approach for recognising and improving the research process is covered in more depth at the end of this section.

Describing the research process allows the sharing of best practise among researchers, prevents researchers making the same mistakes repeatedly, and allows researchers to make a whole bunch of more interesting mistakes. It also provides a training tool for junior researchers, enabling them to learn and replicate how a study should run, and gives senior researchers some rules that they can break in creative and interesting ways.

There are a lot of great books about the basics of running studies (e.g. Steve Krug's Rocket Surgery Made Easy). Some recommendations are covered at the end of this book. In this section we will work through the research process and share guidelines for how to ensure that high quality work occurs at each stage, reducing the opportunity for errors and increasing the impact that a new research team can have.

Starting with research objectives

The research questions, or research objectives, describe, 'what do we want to learn from a round of research?' Some examples could be: "Can users successfully complete the transaction?", "Where are users when they use our app?" or "What are the major challenges users have with ordering a taxi currently?" When working with people new to research, this can be confused with the interview questions that are asked to the participants directly, but they are not the same – directly asking users the question that the study hopes to answer will most often lead to poor quality answers and shallow research findings.

Ensuring that both researchers and the product team members understand the difference between the research objectives and the questions asked is important to avoid confusion between the goals of the study and the method that will be used to answer those goals. Using the term 'research objectives instead of 'research questions is one way to help avoid misunderstanding. Being explicit about the research process is another and starting each study with a recap of the process is sensible.

Answering the right research questions

Researchers are frequently slightly removed from the product decisions being made. Designers, product managers, and developers are responsible for the decisions about how things should work, and the decision-making process will reveal the information that they need to learn from a study. For example, when designing an app to book haircuts, a designer might then start to wonder, "what are the criteria that people consider when making an appointment for a haircut?" Capturing those questions is important to ensure that research studies are relevant, and good research objectives must come from the whole team, and be agreed by all of the decision makers.

It can be tempting for researchers to come up with the research objectives by themselves - this usually feels much easier because it requires no debate, and allows researchers to design the studies that they feel comfortable or interested in running. The risk of coming up with the research objectives autonomously is that a researcher will plan and run a perfect study that answers questions no-one has asked. This will cause the findings to be ignored, and the reputation of research as a discipline will suffer.

Early on, in particular, it is important to ensure that the right research questions are being tackled. Usability testing is performative and encourages teams to watch, and building interest and good-will while the research function is being established is important. However, they may not be the most useful studies that can be run - early on in the development of a product, learning "what users do in the real world" can have a lot more impact on a product and informing its development than putting a prototype in front of someone. By taking the appropriate time with product managers to understand the stage of the product and the type of decisions they are making, a researcher can make informed decisions about what the most valuable research questions are to answer.

Watch out for the research method deciding the research question. It is very easy to fall into the trap of thinking "we're going to run some usability testing in our lab, what do we want to learn?" Coming up with the method before the research question is backwards - and leads to compromised research that does not necessarily answer the team's most important questions. To avoid this risk, ensure that the research objectives are captured and agreed before deciding on the appropriate method for answering them. In the next section on research planning a technique for matching methods to research questions is covered.

Coming up with research questions

The first step is to generate a big list of research questions the team has. This can be run as a workshop with the whole product team, with several stages:
- Asking all the participants to think about "what information we need to know to improve our confidence about what to build", and capture these on post-its.
- The whole product team vote on which they feel are the most important to answer first, using a method such as dot voting (allocating each participant three dots to vote with on the post-its).

This then needs to be supplemented by a thorough prioritisation, from the researcher and product manager working together to identify:
- Is research the best way of getting answers to this research question? (As opposed to the work of other teams, such as performance analysts)
- Is there enough time for the team to react to this question being answered by a research study?
- Is this research question about a core feature of the product that will impact a large audience?
- Are there complementary research questions which can all be answered by the same study?

This discussion, and the team's dot votes, can help inform which research questions get allocated to the first study. Many research questions will not fit into this first study - they can get added to a backlog - described later in this section.

The kick-off meeting

Having decided the first set of objectives, a potential research method and timeline can be proposed and added to the kick-off template, described earlier in this book. This can then be used to have a kick-off meeting - where the objectives, a proposed method of answering them, and the dates for the study can be discussed and agreed by the whole team.

This is particularly important, because defining the study objectives is the stage where feedback from the wider product team is most useful and wanted. Without getting agreement on 'what you want to learn', later discussions on 'how should we learn it', are going to be unproductive and the cause of friction between colleagues. The researcher should be clear that they want input and discussion on 'what we're going to learn', but that they decide 'how should we answer it', in order to apply their expertise appropriately.

Having discussed and agreed all the points in the kick-off document, planning the first study can begin.

Capturing research questions in a backlog

Some of the research questions that the team generate in the workshop will not fit into the first study - usually due to requiring a different audience or method to answer. A great method to manage these previously described by Kieron Kirkland when he was at GDS is to create a Trello board.

A research backlog created in Trello can track the status of research questions.

Trello is a project management tool that allows cards to be created and then assigned into categories. By creating a card for each research question, it can be allocated into a category such as:
- In the backlog
- In the next study
- In the current study
- Answered

The order of the cards in the backlog category can be prioritised to indicate which are the most important. This method of tracking research questions also allows teams to follow the research questions that have already been answered, and the findings associated with each research question can be kept in each card's note (such as a link to the report).

Planning research studies

Planning a research study requires a combination of creativity and rigour. It is easiest to be successful when building upon a body of best practice that has been informed by previous mistakes, to avoid making the same mistakes again. During part two of this book we covered the creation of a checklist to ensure that each task is done efficiently and it's during this planning stage where the checklist is most important.

To successfully plan a study requires:
- Making good decisions about the method, participants and dates
- Creating the materials needed to run a study
- Ensuring everything will work as expected

Each of these will be looked at in turn.

Picking a method

The method should always follow the research objectives, and part of the skill of being a researcher is to identify the appropriate method. Having identified the research objectives as part of the kick-off, deciding the appropriate method should be a reasonably mechanical activity:
- For research questions such as "How do people currently...", use methods that explore their existing behaviour, such as observing people in context or interviewing them.
- For research questions such as "Can people do this...", use methods where users are reacting to a task or stimulus, such as usability testing.
- For research questions such as "What do people think about...", use methods that gather opinions, such as surveys or interviews. However, we have to be careful with opinions - as will be covered later in this section.

Unfortunately, there are usually other limitations on the method selection beyond just "what would be the best way of answering this question?" Compromise will often be necessary, because factors such as the budget and time available will impact how the study is conducted. However, to build trust early in a relationship with a product teams, it is important not to hide this - being honest to the product team about the compromises being made, and the impact that may have on the findings will help teams make an informed decision about how they want to proceed.

Having picked the method, it is then important to generate appropriate questions or tasks that will give reliable answers to these questions. A process for doing that is to list all the research questions, assign each to a method, and then generate tasks or questions to answer them.

For example, a selection of research questions for a car-selling website may be:
- *How do people sell their cars currently?*
- *Can they successfully use our website to list their car?*
- *Do they understand how to list as an auction vs fixed price?*
- *What did they think about the experience of using our website?*

Each of these research questions can first be allocated a method
- How do people sell their cars currently? - *Observation or interview*
- Can they successfully use our website to list their car? - *Observation during usability test*
- Do they understand how to list as an auction vs fixed price? - *Observation and probing questions during usability test*
- What did they think about the experience? - *Interview or survey.* This is also not a good question for evidence-based decision making though, as we will cover shortly.

Next the specific prompts and questions that will be asked to the participants for each section can be generated. Question prompts have the goal of fully exploring the topic. Task prompts describe the prompt that will be given to participants as part of the study.

- How do people sell their cars currently? - Observation or interview
    - Question prompts
        - "Tell me about the last time you sold your car"
        - "What made you decide you wanted to sell your car?"
        - "What was the first thing you did to sell your car?"
        - "How did you learn that was the first thing to do?"
        - "How was your experience doing it?"
        - "What did you do next to sell your car?"
        - "Is this the only car you've sold? What did you do differently to the previous time?"
        - etc...
- Can they successfully use our website to list their car? - Observation during usability test
    - Task:
        - You have heard that there is a website called listmycar.com and decide you want to sell your car on it. You have taken a photo of your car for the listing and know the make and model. Please list the car on the website for a price you'd be happy to receive.
- Do they understand how to list as an auction vs fixed price? - Observation and probing questions during usability test
    - Questions after the car is listed:
        - How much have you listed your car for?

- How did you know that you'd listed it for that much?
        - Was there any other way you could have priced your car?
        - How did you know that there was another way?
  - What did they think about the experience? - Interview or survey.
    - Questions
      - What did you think about using the website?
      - Did anything stand out as particularly good?
      - Did anything stand out as particularly bad?
    - Ratings
      - How easy or difficult was it to list a car on the website today? (rated on a Likert scale)

Going through all of the research objectives, assigning methods, and generating questions and tasks, a basic outline for the study emerges and the researcher has confidence they will address all of the objectives.

What's the problem with opinions?

In the first part of this book, we talked about the importance of educating the product teams. Something that is important to reiterate often with teams new to research is the dangers of confidently drawing conclusions about what action to take on data that is unreliable or unsafe. Opinion data is one of the riskiest areas in which this could occur, because it looks easy to interpret ("people said they liked this, so it must be a good idea").

One of the issues with using opinions from the qualitative studies is that they are not designed to see how representative the opinions are. We can discover that those opinions exist, and confidently tell teams that, but that is not particularly useful data to inform decisions without knowing whether 1% or 100% of people have that same opinion. Using statistical tools such as adjusted Wald, we can see that the proportions of people who agree with the statement could be wildly different (e.g. if one out of five people said it, that proportion could represent anywhere between 2% and 64% of the wider audience), and so drawing meaning from whether an opinion was given more often than another is meaningless without a quantitative study. Because opinions are about "what do people think?" rather than a binary "can people use it as intended?", it is not sensible to make decisions without a clear direction on what people think - unlike usability issues, where we know that it is 'broken' even if only one person cannot use it as intended, and so action to resolve the issue is appropriate.

Opinion data is often captured on prototype software, which does not represent the intended experience, and captured outside of realistic contexts, which will influence people's opinions, and make the data captured less 'true' if applied to inform decisions about a final product. Capturing people's behaviour is therefore more trustworthy information to inform decisions. Opinion data also does not necessarily correlate with a business's goals - people do not like Facebook tracking their behaviour, but that will not stop Facebook doing it because it is how they make money.

For this reason, to get reliable opinion data requires a different study to most qualitative user research studies, and care must be taken when opinion data is reported from usability or contextual studies.

This risk of not being careful with opinions for a new research team is not only that the organisation will start making decisions based on data that may be untrue, but also that it impacts their trust in the findings from studies where the findings are reliable and should be trusted. Later on, in this section, appropriate ways of dealing with and communicating opinion findings are discussed, to avoid the risk of good quality work being disregarded.

Recruiting participants

As covered in part two, there are a variety of approaches that can be taken to recruit participants for research. The kick-off will have provided information about the type of user, and with the dates agreed, it is now an appropriate time to start recruitment. When working with internal or external recruiters, that is just an email - for ad-hoc participant recruiter, it is time to plan how to find the users and start putting in the work to schedule them.

Timing a study

The recruitment method has the largest impact on how a study runs. When using a participant recruiter, there will be a two-week lead-time between when the study is commissioned, and when it can run - this can be longer with some recruiters, particularly if they are trying to source niche participants.

After the study, some time will be needed for analysis and sharing findings. A schedule for a round of research could look like this:

	DAY 1	DAY 2	DAY 3	DAY 4	DAY 5
WEEK 1	KICK OFF	RECRUIT	TEST PREP	TEST PREP	TEST PREP
WEEK 2					
WEEK 3	PILOT	TEST	ANALYZE	DEBRIEF	TIDY UP

A schedule for a round of research, allowing for a two-week recruitment.

To increase the velocity of research, some overlap can occur between the preparation of one study and the completion of another, like this.

	DAY 1	DAY 2	DAY 3	DAY 4	DAY 5
STUDY 1 WEEK 1	KICK OFF	RECRUIT	TEST PREP	TEST PREP	TEST PREP
STUDY 1 WEEK 2					
STUDY 2 WEEK 1	KICK OFF	RECRUIT	TEST PREP	TEST PREP	TEST PREP
STUDY 1 WEEK 3	PILOT	TEST	ANALYZE	DEBRIEF	TIDY UP
STUDY 2 WEEK 2					
STUDY 2 WEEK 3	PILOT	TEST	ANALYZE	DEBRIEF	TIDY UP

Two rounds of research can be overlapped and run in four weeks.

This gives appropriate time for a researcher to plan, run, and debrief a study. When working in pairs, some of the stages can be briefer - for example, because notes can be captured during the sessions, this reduces analysis time. With more complex research methods, and more complicated data, additional test or analysis days will be required.

The length of a research study does not correlate with a common two week sprint, and it is important not to compromise on running or analysing studies properly, so it is recommended not to try and squish this down into two weeks (for one thing, to keep the participant recruiter happy!).

Writing the study plan and other materials

The goal of the study plan/discussion guide is to ensure that the researcher consistently runs the study successfully and includes all the pre-designed questions and tasks required to answer the research objectives.

In Part 2 of this book, a template for creating study plans was covered.

The study plan template described earlier.

Now the objectives and tasks have been agreed, it is possible to fill this out - with pre-study and post-study interview questions, and the task boxes representing how the tasks will run.

Task:
You have heard that there is a website called listmycar.com and decide you want to sell your car on it.
You have taken a photo of your car for the listing and know the make and model.
Please list your car on the website for a price you'd be happy to receive.

What we'll ask:	**What we'll observe:**	**What we will learn:**
What are you doing now?	Do they successfully upload their car details?	Can they successfully use our website to list their car?
How did you know that was what you were meant to do?	Do they successfully craft the advert?	Do they understand how to list as an auction vs fixed price?
	Do they successfully complete the process?	
	Are they aware they decided between an auction or fixed price advert?	

Post Task Questions:
- How did you find listing the car today?
- Was there anything difficult or confusing about doing it?
- How much have you listed your car for?
- How did you know that you'd listed it for that much?
- Was there any other way you could have priced your car?
- How did you know that there was another way?

Unlike the research objectives covered in the kick-off document, it is sensible to discourage feedback from a wide audience on the discussion guide - the product team will be less experienced in how to craft appropriate tasks and questions to get the correct data from a research study than a researcher, and researchers have specialist skills and experience that should lead to them making better choices about how to frame tasks and questions. However, in the spirit of working openly, researchers should share their discussion guide with their colleagues and be prepared to explain their decisions within it. This becomes more important if the researcher hopes to use notes from the product team to inform their analysis, as will be covered in the final part of this book.

During preparation for a study, other things may also need to be made to support the test including:
- A structured note taking template (which will be covered shortly)
- The consent form
- The task prompts to give to the participant
- The questionnaire/other things intended to be given to the participant

Because many of these will have been templated, the task of creating them should not be overly burdensome.

Running a pilot

There are many things that will go wrong during research sessions. This includes:
- The questions being unclear and getting poor quality responses back
- The prototype failing to work
- The recording failing and the video being lost
- The observation stream cutting out during a session
- The session being too long and having to stop prematurely

- The consent forms not being ready to sign

To help reduce the risk of these issues occurring, it is essential to have a trial run before the study. Things may still go wrong during the real session, but by running a pilot session before hand, some of them can be caught and fixed before real participants turn up, saving the money from a wasted session and keeping the product team happy.

To run a pilot test, find a volunteer who can act the role of the participant. The more distance they have from working on the thing being tested the better job they will do at playing the role. The moderator running the study should run the study for real, as if they are a real participant, to give the opportunity for errors to emerge in the study, the preparation or the technology.

Timing a pilot test is a balancing act between "When is the thing ready to be tested?" and "when do we still have time to fix issues that emerge?" The morning of the day before the study gives enough time to fix most issues that may occur, and the product team can be given a deadline of the day before the pilot to prepare any prototypes required.

After the pilot, remember to review the recordings to check that the sound was on!

Running the study

Running sessions is where the study's data is generated. Having prepared well and run a pilot, there should be no surprises. However, there are still a few areas where careful attention can help improve the quality of the data that is captured from the study and reduce the hassle for the later analysis stages.

The participant experience

The purpose of bringing in real users is to get them to reveal their true behaviour and thoughts to the moderator, uncovering things the moderator was unaware of. If the participant is visiting an unfamiliar place, rather than a researcher going to their home, the participant will be apprehensive and more stressed than they would be in a natural context - this will impact their behaviour and thoughts.

To improve how studies run, curating the end to end participant experience, and ensuring that it is as non-disruptive as possible, will have an impact on the quality of the session. This includes:

- Providing the participants with enough information beforehand, so they know where to go, what will happen when they arrive, who will be meeting them, and what they will be expected to do during the session.
- Looking at how they will be met when they arrive at the building and ensuring that it is pleasant - for example, briefing the front-desk on what to do.
- Ensuring the journey from the front-desk to the session is appropriate - they are offered appropriate refreshments, and the opportunity to go to the toilet, and are not exposed to anything intimidating (like a room full of observers).

- The room the session occurs in is unremarkable and will not influence the participants opinions or behaviour. Keep the many awards the team has won somewhere else!
- The manner of the moderator is friendly and appropriate, and they do not seem like a scary person.

Time spent understanding and designing the experience that participants will have when coming in for research will be valuable for helping get more authentic behaviour and thoughts from them.

Good moderation

The role of the moderator is similar to one of a performer - to create the situations and scenarios that cause the participant to talk honestly about their previous experience, and allow them to react authentically to stimuli such as prototypes. The moderator then must convey the experience the participant is having in the room to a wider audience, of note-takers or observers, so that it can be recorded accurately.

To achieve this requires a performance from the moderator - pretending to be ignorant about what to do or how the software works, to give the participant the opportunity to discover and explain it themselves. Simultaneously, the moderator needs to have perfect awareness of what is happening and how the software works, so that they can ensure the issues occurring are understood and captured correctly, and the causes identified.

The audience for the performance are the observers taking notes, and the moderator has to ensure that the issues are being communicated appropriately to them - for example, by repeating what the participant has said, or asking them to describe and explain their behaviour, and asking probing questions to get the participant to articulate their understanding.

To communicate what is happening to observers, confirming the behaviour that participants are displaying is important - even when the issue seems obvious, the cause can often be misleading. Without knowing what the participant is thinking, it is difficult to distinguish between "the user didn't understand this" and "the user understood this but decided not to do it". Uncovering the root cause of the issue is necessary, because the fix for either of these issues would be different. Because of this, it is important to ask participants questions to uncover their understanding of what is going on - which will also make it easier for the note-taker to capture.

A challenge is asking these questions without changing the participants behaviour. Asking high-level and general questions is one way of ensuring the questions are not leading - asking "what are you doing currently?", in a non-judgemental tone of voice, should get people to explain their goals and thoughts without the moderator giving away any details about what they should be doing. Their answer can inspire follow up questions getting gradually more specific. In contrast, a question like "why did you click on the search page?" reveals to the participant both that they are on the search page, and implies that they are not meant to be there - this then makes it impossible to draw conclusions about what the users understanding was before the question was asked. Users unbiased answers about their understanding or goals are often surprising, which is a great start for interesting findings.

A good method for the moderator to ensure that they are getting enough depth from the interactions is to imagine how it will be reported back to the product team. In order to make appropriate changes, the team will need to know "why the issue occurred". In order to prioritise what to do, the team will need to know "what the impact on the user is". For that reason, feedback such as "This webpage looks confusing" is useless, because it does not contain the details necessary for teams to understand why or decide what to do about it. The moderator constantly has to evaluate the depth of understanding they have received so far, and then go deeper if necessary. With follow up questions and probing, the finding could become *"Users failed to find all of the items listed on the page because the header did not look clickable. The appearance of the header was different to other links on the page and there was no additional indication given it was clickable. Because of that, the user never discovered how to see all of the items currently listed for sale and described the webpage as 'looking confusing'"*.

To ensure that the appropriate level of detail is achieved, the moderator must always be thinking about the data they are gathering in the session and evaluating whether they are getting enough to explain the issue wholly to others without having unresolved questions. When there is a gap, generating and asking appropriate probing questions will help capture enough data.

This clarification is particularly important when opinions are raised by the participant. Because of the known issues with opinions from qualitative studies, the value of them are low (there is not much that can be done with the feedback "I don't like this"). However, usability issues can often be influencing people's opinions, and are sensible findings to communicate from these studies. So, probing on opinions to identify if there are any usability issues behind them will reveal more useful data from a study.

The risk of not getting deep enough data or failing to convey the detail to the note-taker is awkward debriefs when presenting findings to a team. They will have questions that will be impossible to answer, and it will reflect poorly on the quality of the work and the research team. That is not great for a new research team. Even worse are situations where depth is obviously missing, but no-one is asking about it - this implies a lack of interest from the product team, and that the work is considered irrelevant. The best prevention for either of those situations is good quality studies that are finding reliable and useful information from users.

Great note-taking

Having a dedicated note-taker for research sessions can greatly increase the pace that research can run at. The role of the note-taker is to create an accurate record of what occurred, which can be used for analysis. Without having someone doing this live for the sessions, the note-taking has to be done after the sessions have been completed, which adds to the delays before debriefing can happen, and increases the risk that the product team will act before thorough analysis has been conducted and shared.

Ethically, the participant should know that someone is observing and taking notes - as described in the consent form. However, observing from another room or location will help prevent the note-taking from biasing the participants behaviour.

When note-taking, aiming for an unfiltered record of what participants said and did is better than trying to interpret the issues live - because the participant will be broadcasting behavioural data all the time, taking time to analyse during the session will prevent the note-taker from paying attention to what the user is doing. For that reason, it is sensible to capture everything (with time stamps if possible) and filter it after the session is complete.

In order to describe the impact of the issues later, it is important to not only capture the issues that occurred, but also what happened as a result of that issue - did it lead to the participant missing a feature? Did it require moderator intervention, etc. Writing not only 'what happened' but also 'what happened next' allows the impact to be understood and the severity of the issue to be prioritised appropriately.

There are a lot of tools that can be used to capture notes - for example usability tools like Morae allow the notes to be captured alongside the video feed (removing the need for timestamps). My preferred tool is a mind mapping software, like Mind Node or Mindjet.

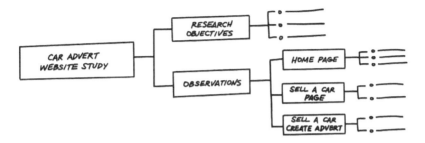

A mind map created in mind mapping software can allow for efficient note taking

A mind map can be pre-prepared with appropriate sections for notes, using the research objectives as a guide. For example, if the objective was "can people use the website to list their car for sale?", a node on the mind map can be created for each page of the website, such as:
- Home Page
- Sell a car landing page
- Sell a car - describe car page
- Sell a car - create advert page
- Sell a car - confirmation page
- Other

As the participant moves through the purchase journey, the notes about their behaviour and issues can be captured in the relevant section of the mind map, making aggregation easier later. New sections can be added on the fly as required during the session. Some tools also allow the notes to be tagged with numbers, which can be used to capture the participant ID, allowing all the notes from all sessions to be captured on the same map without losing the ability to trace notes back to the original participant. This will also speed up analysis later.

As a note taking method, using mind maps take a while to learn and become familiar enough with to use to capture notes live. However, the speed benefits for analysis can make it well worth the time investment to learn and practice. We will cover analysis next.

Efficient analysis

Studies generate a huge amount of data - a quantity that is overwhelming for a product team to interpret and act from. Analysis is the stage where all the raw data collected during a study gets looked at, and the meaning extracted. Once again, a structured process can help make this manageable and quick.

A process for analysing findings

Having completed the data collection part of a study, it is time to uncover the answers to the research questions. Affinity mapping is a popular technique for doing this with the findings of qualitative research - using clustering techniques to expose the themes behind the information that was learned during the study.

The first step is to atomise the notes from the study so that each unit (post-it, bullet point, or node depending on what format the notes are captured in) contains only a single observation. For example, if the raw note had said, "this user gets stuck on the payment screen because they did not see the confirmation button and also did not know how much it would charge them", this contains two issues (the confirmation button and the price), so should be split into two. Some formats for note-taking, such as post-its or using a mind map make it simple to do this - often the notes are captured in the appropriate format already. Other methods of note-taking, like a long word document transcribing what was said, will require more work to split into individual observations. This process will require moving these observations around, and so a format that makes moving observations simple (like post-its or a mind map) will save a lot of time.

Post-its describing one observation per post-it

Now having made all the individual observations into a format that can be manipulated, it is time to start grouping them. Grouping can be done in a number of ways, and the correct way depends on the audience - for example, a researcher may consider grouping by the nature of the issue (e.g. 'visual', 'interaction') if the team working on it are going to split the actions by discipline. Other ways of grouping can include by topic when analysing interviews, or by webpage when looking at the data from a usability test. Using the research objectives as a guide and being open to adding or changing groupings as themes emerge is the best approach.

To start, take the first observation and assign it to an existing pre-defined group (as described above), or create a new group if it does not map to one that exists already. Then take a second observation and think about whether it is similar to the first. If it is, put them together. If not, find or make an appropriate group for it.

Similar post-its should be grouped together

Repeat this for all the observations. Some observations will not be relevant to the research objectives, and so can be discarded. When all the observations have been assessed, it will have revealed some clusters of observations around some topics. Make sure all the clusters are named to describe how they are similar.

Next, it is time to evaluate each cluster in turn. Return to each observation within the cluster, and identify whether the observations describe the same thing, or describe a different finding about the same subject. Combine those that are the same. Depending on the goals of the study, the points will either be describing user's behaviours or motivations in the real world (e.g. "The reason this person last bought a car was because they had had a child") or about their experience using the product being tested ("Participant 4 didn't see the confirmation button"). Once all have been assessed and duplicates identified, each observation should be re-written (and the raw data reviewed) to ensure they can be fully explained in a way that is helpful for the product team.

For usability issues, ensuring that the cause (what it was about the system that made this happen) and the impact (what did that do to the participant's ability to use the system) is very helpful to achieve this. For example:

The participant was unable to complete their purchase:
- *Cause: The confirmation button did not have appropriate contrast against the background*
- *Impact: Users did not see the button, so failed to identify how to complete their purchase. They then went back to the checkout and were unable to complete the purchase of their intended item.*

For describing user's behaviour in the real world, ensuring that the 'why' is explained will help ensure the information can be applied by teams usefully.

Life events are one trigger of buying cars
- *Participants described that major life events, such as having children or getting a new job were a cause for them to consider buying a new car*
- *They described several reasons for this. Some were practical (e.g. getting enough space to include an extra child, or better mileage when having to drive further for a new job)*
- *Other reasons described were reflective - the life event had triggered them to consider their priorities and had made them consider getting a new car to reflect their status.*

Using affinity mapping to interpret qualitative data is an effective technique for ensuring all the data is evaluated and communicated appropriately and with enough depth.

More Mind Maps

In the previous chapter, we described the benefits of mind maps for note-taking. It is also a great tool for the analysis process and can decrease the analysis time significantly.

Having captured the raw notes against sections from the discussion guide, as described in the note-taking section, it is ready to be used for analysis.

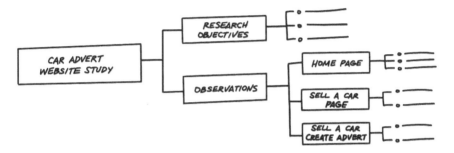

The raw notes are initially captured against the part of the site they occurred on

First, make a duplicate of all the notes, to prevent raw notes accidentally being deleted. Then create a blank section for the analysed notes.

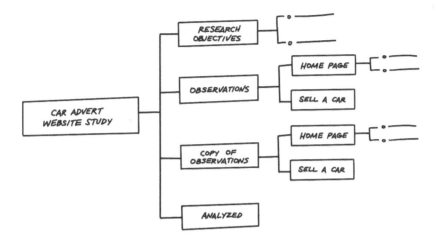

Duplicating the observations can provide a back-up if data is accidentally lost during analysis.

Then in turn, cut each individual observation from the raw notes, evaluate whether it is relevant, and paste it into the analysed notes section. Look at the existing notes in that section to decide where it should go. The mind mapping tool can be used to create appropriate sections for grouping as they become evident. As described earlier, sensible ways to group the issues depend on the context of the product team being presented too - consider what grouping would make it simple for the product manager to hand over responsibility for resolving the issues to other team members - potentially by discipline, or by section of the product.

This can then be repeated until all the notes are copied down into the appropriate section. Then each section in turn can be investigated in more depth, describing the issues within it, describing the causes and impacts and keeping the raw notes attached if tracing back to the participant is required.

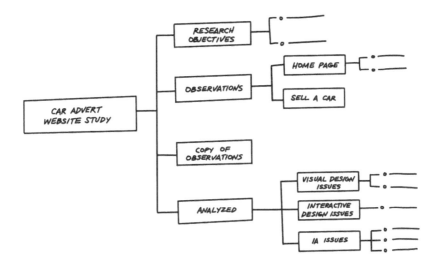

The observations can then be re-sorted into sections that are meaningful for the product team and rewritten appropriately.

When sorted, the mind map can be used to present a quick debrief without the need for a presentation to be created, useful if time is short. Some mind mapping tools can also export into data formats that can be imported into presentations via scripts, greatly reducing the effort required to make slides for a debrief.

Collaborative Analysis

One of the challenges researchers face is that they are not the ones who have to make decisions about how things work – instead, their studies inform the work of designers, product managers and the rest of the team. The role of the researcher is therefore not just to run the study, but also ensure that the team understand the findings and are able to take sensible decisions based on them.

One of the communication tools available to researchers is to involve the whole product team in analysis. The pros and cons of this is explored in more depth in part four of this book, where a practical approach to collaborative analysis is described in full.

Although this method of analysis takes more time, and increases the risk of dubious quality findings being generated, it exposes the team to the raw data on a more direct level than just observing research sessions, and can help them understand their users better - so can be appropriate for organisations who are sufficiently mature with their research practise to avoid the risks.

Rating issues

Having identified some usability issues, either by individual or collaborative analysis, another useful communication tool available to researchers is to rate the severity of issues. This method of rating is only relevant when communicating usability issues (when the user didn't experience the system as intended), rather than for studies about the audience's behaviour and motivations in the real world.

The benefit of rating the severity of usability issues is that it helps the team prioritise and decide what to deal with first. It is not a judgement of the product team's abilities - ensuring that they understand the presence of high severity issues is not reviewing their performance will help avoid conflict.

One popular way of rating the severity of issues is the scale described on the website userfocus, in their article 'how to prioritise usability problems'. David Travis, the author of the article describes a 4-point scale for issues: critical, high, medium and low. In addition to these, consider adding 'positive' as a tag to describe things that worked as designed - the benefit of capturing features that work is that it lets teams know what they should not be changing, or hint towards future design patterns.

A structured way of categorising issues is important to increase objectivity and team's trust in their researcher. The method described involves asking these questions:

- Does the issue occur on a critical path that the user must take?
- Does the issue occur persistently?
- Is the issue difficult to overcome?

For some types of software, identifying the critical path can be obvious - for example, booking a taxi in a taxi booking app. In cases where it is not clear what the primary and secondary functionality is, it can be a beneficial thing to cover in the kick-off meeting - long before it is needed to assess the issues. Identifying these prior to the study running decreases the risk of bias based on seeing the sessions and trying to 'game' the severity rating.

Identifying whether the issue is persistent is frequently misunderstood as meaning 'does this happen for multiple users?'. We will look at why that's not safe to draw conclusions from shortly. Instead the actual meaning of this question is "once a user has overcome this issue once, can they avoid it occurring a second time?'. Users can avoid learnable issues, but some issues are impossible to prevent occurring and will fail this criterion.

To define 'difficult to overcome' in a consistent way, consider whether the moderator had to help them or whether the user was able to overcome the issue without assistance or going to the internet for help. To apply this method requires consistent moderation to ensure that the moderator does not step in prematurely.

Give each issue a point for each question is answered 'yes'. Then add up those points to arrive at the rating:

3 points - Critical issue

2 points - High issue

1 point - Medium issue

0 points - Low issue

And positive issues are those where a feature worked as intended. To identify these, review the research objectives, and note which ones 'passed' with no associated usability issues. In order to add insight and help share best practice, remember to describe what it was about the implementation of those features that caused users to experience them as intended.

Explaining what the ratings mean, and that a standardised process was used to reach them, can help build trust from product teams in the rigour behind the research process, and make them more likely to act on the issues discovered.

Why not count 'how many times did that happen'?

Teams will often ask about how many times an issue occurred. There are a couple of reasons this occurs - it can be an attempt to prioritise the most important issues, or as a method of disregarding unpopular issues.

In the prioritisation method described above 'how many times did the issue happen?' is not one of the factors for deciding whether an issue is important or not. This is because it is not a reliable method of deciding what is important from running a qualitative study.

Industry convention is that a usability study with five users offers a suitable trade-off between the number of issues detected and time taken to run. These qualitative studies offer valuable information about the issues that are observed, prove that these issues exist, and allow many large issues to be identified and understood enough to fix them - making them a good use of researcher time.

However, these studies do not see enough participants to draw statistically significant conclusions about how often these issues would occur in the real world. There is a statistical test that demonstrates this - adjusted Wald can be used to calculate how many times an issue would occur in the real world based on how many times it occurs in a study.

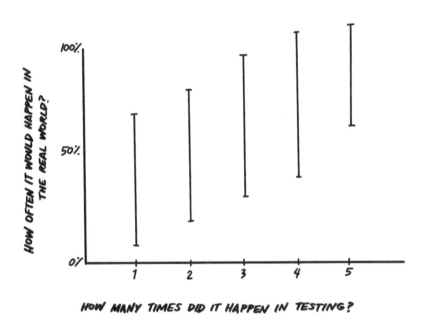

The adjusted Wald graph. The true value showing how often the issue could occur in the real world can be anywhere within the confidence intervals - indicating significant overlap.

The graph shows that an issue that we see once in the study could occur for up to 65% of people in the real world. On the other hand, an issue that occurs for 4 out of 5 users may only occur for 36% of people in the real world - potentially less than the issue we saw occur only once.

This means that if the team was using 'how often it occurred in the study' as a way of prioritising, they might be drawing an incorrect conclusion about which issue would occur more in the real world - because the study was not designed to learn that. It is therefore not a safe way to prioritise.

It would be possible to see more participants to get better information about how often an issue might occur but this is often a bad use of researcher time - having identified that the issue exists, doing something to fix it is sensible, and prioritisation can be done through other methods - as discussed previously. For this reason, when a usability issue is discovered, because it's a defect from the intended experience and we know it exists, it's appropriate to take action even if only one user encountered this issue.

On opinions

As covered when planning a study, opinions are different from usability findings or findings about user behaviour. We saw with the adjusted Wald graph that these qualitative studies are unlikely to tell us much about the representativeness of each thing that occurs or is said. For usability issues where we know something is broken, not knowing representativeness is fine, because each issue is a defect from the intended experience hence it is worth addressing. For understanding user behaviour, combining a quantitative and qualitative study would be sensible, to uncover what behaviour exists then see how prevalent the behaviour is. However, for opinions, we should be careful about how they are treated - people's stated opinions are subject to a lot of biases based on the context in which they are asked and are not safe data for informing decision making.

For this reason, when analysing the findings from qualitative studies, ensure that user opinions are recognised, kept separate from the usability findings, and dealt with separately in the debrief - if reported at all.

Debriefing findings

Communication is a key part of what a user research team will be required to do. In most situations, user researchers are not decision makers and will not be the ones who must decide what to do as a result of some research findings - that will often fall to product or design colleagues. However, the researcher is likely the person who understands best what was learned from a study and what this might mean. Therefore, sharing that knowledge with decision makers is a necessary step for any study to have an impact, and for the value of running user research to be recognised.

This is particularly important with deep strategic research, where storytelling skills and building a narrative around the findings are essential to getting people to care – creating artefacts such as journey maps and other visual representations of findings will help communicate what was learned. However even for standard usability testing, clear communication is important and report structure can help with that.

Debriefing to product teams

The primary audience for evaluative research findings is the team that are working on the thing being researched. This includes UI and UX designers, developers, product managers, content designers, and other people who need to react directly to the findings of a research study.

An effective way of debriefing to this audience is to present the findings in a workshop format. The first half of this workshop runs through an overview of the issues, covering each in enough depth to ensure that people understand what was learned, what caused that behaviour or motivation to occur, and what the impact is. The goal from this overview is to ensure that the team have understood the issues appropriately and accurately and are in the best possible place to make decisions based on them. A format for this presentation is covered imminently.

The second half of this session is interactive and intended to help teams think about actions they could take in reaction to the findings, while ensuring the oversight and understanding a researcher has based on running to the study is still incorporated. A format for this is discussed in the next section on recommendations.

A full debrief using both parts should be scheduled for 1.5-2 hours, and involves all the relevant members of a product team - presenting only to a single member of the team, such as a product manager will increase the potential for miscommunication and misunderstanding as the findings are communicated to others.

What's in a user research report

The report must achieve two aims. It not only has to be a document that can be presented from, but it also has to contain enough information that an audience who reads it after the workshop would take the correct understanding from it (although we will look at more advanced ways of storing research findings long-term later). If blessed with time, creating two separate reports for these audiences can be done – however product teams who observe research sessions will start thinking about changes immediately, and so a prompt and efficient debriefing method increases the opportunity for a research team to influence the changes.

The example that follows is from a fake usability test for an app to help people find somewhere to buy ice-cream, but the format works for other forms of studies.

Title Page

> # Ice-Cream Finder Prototype
>
> Usability Test Report
> February 2020
> Steve Bromley

The title page contains the core information about the study – the subject, the date, the reviewer, the method.

Exec Summary

> # Exec Summary
>
> This round looked at the first prototype of the 'find my ice-cream' app, to identify if people could successfully complete the find ice-cream journey.
>
> Although users were able to understand the proposition of the app, we saw issues when attempting to complete the 'find ice-cream' journey, including that the final 'directions' step was missed because users didn't recognise the finding journey wasn't complete, and difficulty finding how to sort the results page due to the low prominence of the buttons.
>
> We also identified some usability issues with the registration process which will impact the quality of the data captured about users, and the recommendations they will be served in future.

Not everyone will be reading the whole report, and adding an executive summary can help time-poor people evaluate whether reading the full details are worth their time. Here it includes what the scope of the test is, and some of the key findings of the study.

Objectives and Method

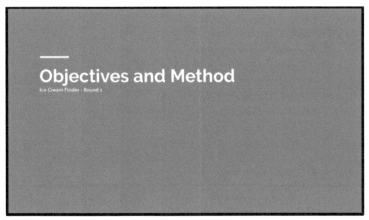

Framing the research by explaining "what did we want to learn?" and "how did we learn it?" can help prevent misunderstandings and answer common questions that the product team will have. The report starts with a section that explains what we wanted to learn from the research, how the research was run, and introduces the prioritisation key used throughout the rest of the report.

> **Context**
>
> Having previously interviewed people and understood some of the issues people have when visiting seaside towns, some potential app ideas have been developed.
>
> This is the first round of research looking at a prototype for a new app to understand if people are able to use it to find ice cream.

Some context on why the study has been run will be helpful for audiences in the future. This will allow them to understand why the study was run, if the original team moves on or people forget.

> **Research Objectives**
>
> Can new users successfully set up their account?
>
> Can users successfully use the app to find ice-cream?
> - Do they discover how to search for ice-cream near them?
> - Do they understand all of the criteria for selecting the best place?
> - Can they successfully follow the directions to find the ice-cream?
>
> What usability issues do they encounter, and do they prevent people from finding ice-cream?

For this specific review, the objectives are very broad – identify usability issues that prevent the app from being experienced as intended. For a real study, the researcher will have met with the developers before running a review to understand what specific research questions they had, based on the project's current priorities, as discussed in the previous sections.

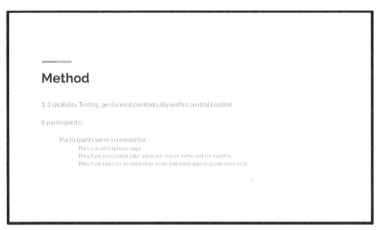

Other product team members won't be as familiar with research methods as the user researcher is, and so some explanation of the method is useful to explain how the review was conducted. When presenting, this is an opportunity to educate people by recapping why this method is appropriate for these research objectives.

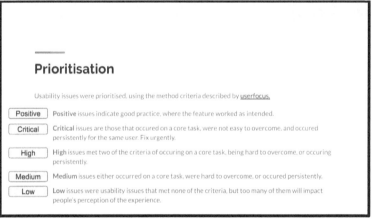

Prioritisation of issues is important in order to help developers decide which issues need their imminent attention, and which can go on the backlog, as previously covered. A method for prioritisation was covered earlier, and it is important to explain the priorities to the product team.

Caveats

This is a **usability study** designed to look at people's behaviour and ability to complete the tasks provided.

It will uncover aspects of the app which people failed to understand, found hard to do or failed to complete. These issues are likely to negatively impact people's opinions and likelihood to use the app, and resolving them will help the app be experienced as designed.

However this type of study does not provide reliable opinion data about whether people **like the app** or **would use it in real life**. Other research studies should supplement this one if these are important objectives.

Honesty about the limitations of the study is important for building research maturity and trust in the work of the research team. A slide to help explain what the implications of the method choice are will help the product team take appropriate action from the findings.

Usability Findings

A section divide to segue into covering the findings from this study. When presenting, this is usually where people start paying attention.

Positives

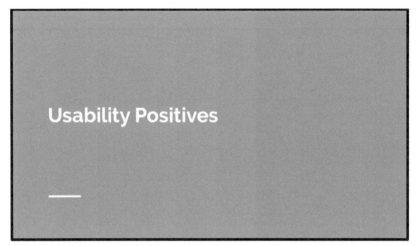

Starting the report with things that worked well has two advantages. Not only does it help the product team identify which features were implemented well and worked as expected (so they know what not to change), but it is also a nice ice breaker when presenting the findings to the product team, especially because bad news usually follows.

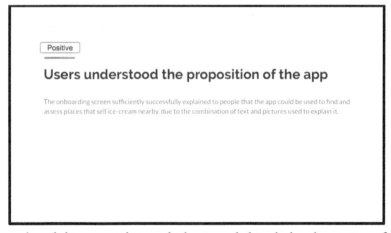

For each usability aspect that worked as intended, include a description of what it was that worked, an explanation of why it worked, and details of the impact on the user's experience as a result of it working. Screenshots can help make it clear which aspect is being described where appropriate.

In this example, only a few positives are in this section currently. There are other positive findings in the report, but they are related to some of the issues identified, so they have been grouped with relevant issues.

Usability Issues

The usability issues are grouped by theme. This makes it both easier to present (because similar items are covered at the same time), and easier for the product team to deal with. Often different members of the product team will be responsible for different aspects of the software, and so splitting the findings into topics helps focus the findings for the right people.

The groups are prioritised, so those with the most severe issues within it appear first.

Another usability positive, as indicated by the icon. This could have been put in the 'usability positives' section, however, because it was relevant to this group of issues about searching for ice-cream journey, it made more sense to present it within this group.

As with the other usability positive, the slide includes details of what the feature being discussed it, why it is experienced as intended by users, and the impact that this has on the user's experience.

> **High**
>
> ## It was not possible to set an appropriate search area
>
> Cause:
> - The search radius is defined by a circle around a central point.
> - Users described that there were areas that were geographically close where they would not visit an ice-cream parlour, due to safety concerns, or a large slope
>
> Impact:
> - Users received lots of results which were irrelevant to them, and needed to manually assess each individual option to identify which were in an appropriate area.
>
> Intent:
> - Users are able to set an appropriate search zone that matches the area they would consider travelling too, and receive results which match that area.

The first actual usability issue. Some things to notice about this slide:

- The issue has been prioritised, as indicated by the icon, and the most severe issues appear first.
- The causes – the reasons the issue occurs – has been included and specifically described.
- The impact – how does this issue affect users – has also been specifically described.
- The design intent has been articulated. This is the success criteria which creates a shared understanding of what this feature is trying to achieve. Defining these can encourage positive communication between the designer and the researcher.
- There is no recommendation for how to resolve the issue. The intent is to address 'what action should be taken as a result of this issue' in the second half of the debrief workshop instead.

A second issue about the same topic, which has been grouped with it. For some issues it's appropriate to include a screenshot to help explain the issue. In this case, unfortunately the app doesn't really exist, and so screenshots aren't possible!

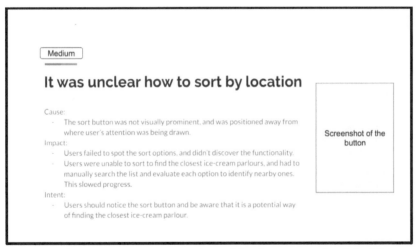

This is a medium priority issue, as indicated by the icon on the slide. This was reached using the prioritisation flow described earlier - the issue is neither persistent or a primary task needed to get ice-cream, so is lower priority than the previous findings.

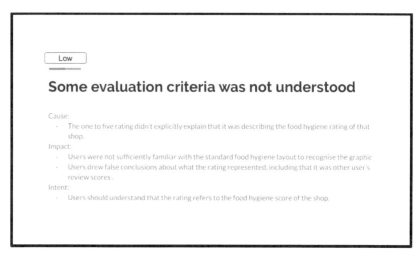

The final issue in this group, and then onto a second group.

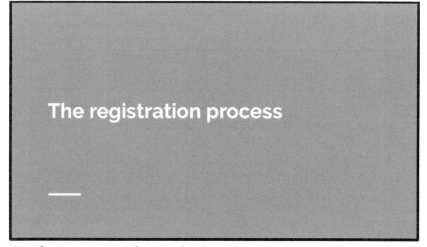

Time for a new group of issues, this time about registration – so, the title for this group summarises the issues within it.

This positive issue is about registration, so has been grouped with the other registration issues, rather than in the positive findings section.

As evident in this slide, an issue can have multiple causes and impacts. When it does, they should be ordered by 'most impactful', but all should be listed.

The workshop

As covered in the next section, instead of making recommendations, using a workshop to help inspire design ideas can often lead to better decisions. If presenting the slides, this section can be used to describe and facilitate the workshop portion.

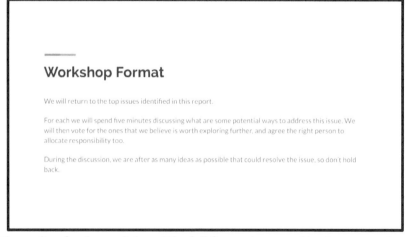

The outline for the workshop. The full format is covered in the next section of this book.

The end of the report

After listing all the usability issues, and discussing potential solutions, the report then covers what will happen after the study.

The next step slide suggests re-reviewing the findings after changes have been made. This reinforces that user research is an iterative process, and a single round of research is not enough – without re-reviewing the software, the product team will not know if they have addressed the usability issues.

> **Thank You!**
>
> Any questions, please drop us an email researchteam@company.com
>
> Previous reports can be found on the team's intranet site.

The report finishes with some contact details, so if the report gets forwarded beyond the original audience, the researcher can be contacted. This would also be a good place to link people to find other reports.

As described, this document is brief enough that it can be presented - but also can be read by a later audience who will be able to understand what the study learned.

Making recommendations

The point of a study is to act based on what is learned. This means that it is necessary to translate what was learned from the study into decisions. Some researchers decide to achieve this by making recommendations with their findings - explaining what the team should do to fix the issues they have identified. Because the researcher was directly involved in the study, saw the users directly, and performed the in-depth analysis of the issues, they have a deeper understanding of the cause and symptoms of issues that occurred than any other member of the team.

However, researcher recommendations can be limited - compared to development, design and product specialists, a researcher will have less knowledge of the limitations of the medium - including what's technically possible, what's been tried before and what the business goals are. To ensure that all of this expertise is taken into account when deciding what action to take, a collaborative workshop can be a successful approach instead of prescribing researcher recommendations.

The second part of a debrief can therefore be a workshop on potential actions. This can also be run from the mind map or done via post-its. The process is as follows:
- Identify the top issues to discuss (prioritising issues makes this simple - just start from the highest priority)
- For each top issue, have a 5-minute discussion generating potential ways to resolve the issues.
- The researcher (or a friend) note-takes all the ideas generated.
- Then review each issue and its proposed solutions, and the group votes on which solutions they believe are worth exploring further.
- The issue is then assigned to a suitable person for further work, based on the area it covers (e.g. whether if it's a UI issue, a product issue, etc.)

At the start of the workshop, explain the rules to the participants about idea generation.
- Each idea generated is to be written down.
- The idea is to generate a high volume of potential ideas - discussion should be positive and there are no bad ideas.
- This workshop is not a commitment to doing the potential resolution discussed. If it turns out to be silly on further investigation, then other solutions will be found.

At the end of this workshop, the preferred potential fixes can be added to the report and distributed to a wider audience. This format ensures that everyone (including the researcher) has the chance to contribute to and evaluate potential resolutions and reduces the risk of important knowledge that the researcher gained in the session not being communicated.

Sharing information with a wider audience

In addition to the immediate audience for a study of decision makers, there is usually a secondary audience of people who want to know about the research that is occurring. This can include senior management, who want reassurance that work is on-track. It can also include other product teams whose work overlaps the subject matter of the study. For this reason, being open and explicit about what research is occurring can be very beneficial - reducing duplication of work and justifying the organisation's investment in research.

Ensuring that the findings from research are discoverable and understandable are important to allow this secondary audience access to the research findings and increases the potential impact of the work a research team does.

To make research discoverable requires several approaches. Using public spaces is an important part - such as a Kanban board showing studies coming up, in flight and recently completed, and the exec summary slides from those that have been completed recently, as well as signposting people towards where they can find more information.

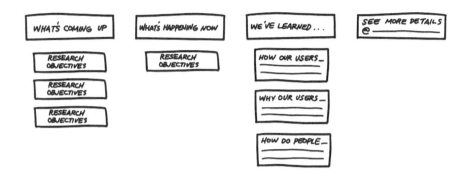

Public displays can help socialise what studies are coming up, occurring currently, and have recently finished.

Using public spaces is best combined with an open digital space to store previous research findings, such as WordPress or google sites. This can combine information about how to engage with the team, and background on how the research team can help, with an accessible list of previous work the team has done, to which new reports will be uploaded after each debrief.

This list should include information that helps other teams assess whether the report from that round of research is relevant to them and worth reading, such as:
- The date of the study
- The objectives of the study
- The type of users who took part
- An exec summary of what was learned
- Links that allow the reader to learn more about the study - e.g. a link to the report, video clips and other artefacts generated by the study.

Using the public space and the digital site as a shop-front for the user research team can help people discover the work done by the research team and increase understanding of the team and its work, in addition to making it possible for the reach of a research study to have an impact beyond its original context. Long after all the original researchers have left, the value of an open store of previous research findings will continue to be felt, and future researchers will be thankful that this was in place from the start.

The importance of honesty

Every research study has limitations. The methodology chosen will impact the conclusions from a study, and the contexts in which those findings are valid. For example:

- Learning achieved in the lab may not accurately reflect real life behaviour.
- Relying on participants recollection or self-reported behaviour is open to significant bias.
- Most qualitative studies are not looking for the representativeness of behaviour, just its existence.
- Participants behaviour and opinions are influenced by the stimulus they are provided - artificial tasks and prototypes will change what people do.

For this reason, including caveats when debriefing is very important - being open about the limitations of the study and the extent to which the findings are safe or can be actioned. This is most pertinent when sharing opinions discovered during a study, because it is most at risk of being challenged (everyone has opinions!). If the decision is made to share opinions discovered in qualitative studies, be sure to reiterate the limitations. This should include that the study has discovered these opinions exist, but other opinions may also exist that contradict these, and to what extent a wider population agree with either opinion is impossible to tell from qualitative research. This also applies to ratings from small studies - make sure to calculate the confidence intervals and explain that the true value could fall anywhere within those.

The reason to be open about the limitations of studies is because of trust. The risk of not being open about the limitations of each study is that if an unsubstantiated finding is challenged by someone outside the team, validly, trust in all of the findings is damaged, and even the valid conclusions from research studies get ignored. This makes it harder for the research team to have an impact. Trust takes a long time to build and is quickly broken!

Honesty is also important in conveying the severity of any issues discovered during usability testing. It can be tempting to downplay the impact of findings, to spare the product team's feelings. This benefits no-one in the long term, because it means that important issues go unresolved and the product's quality decreases. Conversely, it can also be tempting to exaggerate the impact of issues, in order to make the study feel justified or valuable. This hyperbole rapidly impacts people's perceptions of how trustworthy research findings are and will also damage the research team's ability to be listened to and have an impact long term. For this reason, following a repeatable process for deciding severity, as described previously, helps build trust.

Balancing haste and extensiveness

A challenge when debriefing is ensuring that results get back to the team promptly. A researcher could spend weeks making diagrams, highlight videos and beautiful slides. However, throughout that time the rest of the product team are making decisions, and any time spent producing lovely representations of research data will mean those decisions are being made without access to that data.

This is particularly relevant for the research studies evaluating work that has been done - timely debriefing ensures that the information from the study can feed into iterative work promptly before the team's focus moves elsewhere. There is more leeway for a longer analysis and debrief time with larger strategic pieces of research about understanding the audience, because that knowledge can be applied throughout the development process.

Despite the need for haste, some time is needed to perform analysis and decide how to communicate the findings, otherwise the team will be making decisions based on poorly interpreted data. This is the same problem as product teams diving straight into making changes based on observing a research session, rather than waiting for a researcher to present the analysed findings.

For this reason, a balance between haste and rigour is required. For a typical usability test, the following schedule might be appropriate:

- Last Test Day + 1 - Analysis of the raw data, grouping and rewording to ensure the issues are explained accurately.
- Last Test Day + 2 - Putting the issues into the report template, presenting it and running the debrief workshop with the team.
- Last Test Day + 3 - A final pass of the report, adding screenshots to explain the issues and the potential resolutions generated in the workshop, before sending this around to the team and the wider audience.

This schedule helps balance the tensions between haste and accuracy, and ensures that the product team aren't waiting too long to get the results. This reduces the chance that they will act prematurely based on their own conclusions, but also gives some the researcher time after the initial debrief to make the report appropriate for a wider audience.

Continual iteration

While the team is new, there will be a lot of things that go wrong during the planning and execution of a research study, and it is unlikely that each stage will have gone as smoothly as this section of the book implied. The end of a study is a great time to reflect on this, identify actions to be taken, and help ensure that the research process is continually iterating and evolving.

A format for this could be for the researchers involved in the study to individually reflect on each stage (kick off, preparation, running the study, analysis, debrief) and identify things that went particularly well during this study, and problems that occurred in the planning and running of the study. The focus of this reflection is to consider the process of running research, rather than the issues discovered about the product being tested.

After individually identifying points, a joint 30-minute session with all the researchers can discuss each of these and incorporate the things that went well into shared practice - e.g. documenting them in the checklist or team knowledge store (as covered in part two).

Things that did not go well should also be discussed, and the research team can decide what action would be appropriate to stop this issue occurring again. These can then become team tasks, as will be covered in part four of this book.

By embedding this practice of reflecting on how research works and iterating it, the team can share best practice amongst the researchers and help everyone get better at their jobs. This process also actively identifies and overcome issues, which continues to improve the service they are offering to the organisation - helping to integrate research and ensure its continued success, moving from a fragile new user research team to a core part of how products are developed.

Part 4:

After the beginning

Building User Research Teams

Having successfully run some studies, the research team's priorities slowly move from forming a team to embedding research as a core discipline, expanding its reach and influence. A rigorous process for running research, as covered in the previous section, is important for starting to build trust, and demonstrate that user research studies can provide useful and accurate information for the development of products. However, this is only the beginning, and as a research team's maturity grows, so do the tasks that they should be thinking about.

In this section, some of the important areas to focus on to ensure the team's continued growth are covered, including:
- Team tasks to optimise the research process
- Generating demand for research
- Expanding the methods a research team can apply
- Hiring new researchers
- Collaborative practice within research
- Promoting the re-use of research findings

By gradually incorporating each of these into how the team develops, a new research team can embed itself as part of the organisation and become a core part of how products are made.

Team tasks

Sometimes there are down times when there are no studies to run. This can be due to bad luck with scheduling, a test falling through, or the gap between participant recruitment kicking off and the study beginning. During that time, it can be a challenge to find something to do that is productive and beneficial for the team. For a new team, this can be a really valuable period to help focus on research practice and find areas to improve, particularly the invisible parts of the process that do not involve direct contact with participants. This process of compartmentalising, reflecting on, and improving how the process of research works is the essence of research-ops, which has become recognised as a separate practice over the last few years, but has always been important for research teams to perform.

Team tasks are discrete bits of work that help improve how the research team functions. This can include:

- Creating a template for a common task that people do often, such as standard formats for a questionnaire, or a debrief template
- Automating an aspect of reporting, such as creating graphs from ratings
- Documenting how something works, so that new team members can do it
- Engaging a new supplier
- Improving how the research team's work is accessed or understood by colleagues
- Creating presentations to educate the organisation or other researchers
- Optimising the technical setup of the research lab
- Implementing and piloting a new research methodology

They will often be generated by the post-study reflection on how a previous round of research went, as described earlier in the continual iteration part of this book. This can include looking at the good practice that an individual has done and creating a way for that practice to be disseminated amongst the team. It will also include taking actions which prevent problems recurring that emerged during the execution of a previous test.

The benefits for the team are obvious. By overcoming problems that a researcher has encountered and sharing good practice, the whole team improves, and studies become easier to run, more efficient, and more accurate - leading to the quality of the team's work improving overall.

For an individual there are also benefits - besides being nice to their colleagues, it also offers development opportunities to move from an individual contributor to taking ownership of part of the development of the research team and how it works. Introducing this variety in the role beyond just running different kinds of research studies helps people build their own skills and grow - offering new challenges and hopefully retaining them for longer.

An appropriate way of tracking these team tasks, like many other activities done by the research team, is a Kanban board. The backlog will be populated by the post-study reflecting meetings, and then can be claimed by individuals who are interested in doing something about that task. When complete, it can be moved into the 'done' pile, which can then be shared at a team meeting so that everyone knows the process change or work that has been done. After sharing the change with the whole team, it can be considered complete and removed from the board.

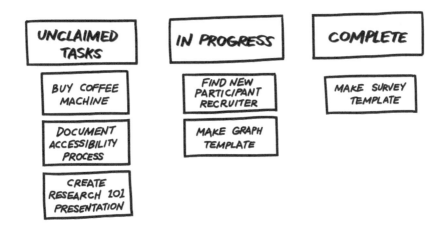

Tracking team tasks

By generating and executing team tasks, downtime between or during studies is no longer unproductive, and will continue to help the team evolve.

Generating a demand for research

Until making decisions based on the findings of user research becomes a standard way of working for product teams, a new research team must be proactive in finding things to work on. The best way to show the benefits of user research is through demonstrating value, hence proactively sourcing work from product teams and then delivering to a high quality will help ensure the long-term success of the team.

Start by creating a list of products and features being worked on, and the responsible people from each product team who make decisions that impact the implementation of them (such as the product manager, designer, content writers). Meeting with each of them, talking about the current stage of their product, what they are worried about, and the decisions they will have to make will reveal potential research questions, which can then be captured, prioritised, and answered with studies from the user research team.

Some factors to consider for deciding what the highest priority thing to work on include:

Is a research study the appropriate way to answer the questions the product team have?
Some research questions can often be requests for 'decisions' in disguise, and teams are hoping for a study to tell them exactly what choice to make. This can result from a lack of confidence that the decision makers have in their own decisions. This can be hard to manage; giving information to inform decisions is the job, but good decisions also consider factors other than user behaviour - such as the business goals, and what is technically feasible. An important part of the education a new research teams should share is setting expectations with product managers and designers that the results of any single study are unlikely to give a definitive answer on how to proceed, and that decisions are still needed.

Is the product team in a position to react to the findings of a study?
When evaluating potential research studies, ensure that the product team have time to act based on the results of the study. When research is commissioned without a plan for 'what will we do with the results', it is often a sign that the research is performative - being run to show that research is being run, rather than actually informing real decisions.

Do the research questions relate to an area of high importance to the business?
When there are multiple potential topics that a research study could answer. Working closely with product managers to prioritise them by importance to the business goals will help ensure that the studies a research team run have a high impact.

Are there assumptions informing big decisions that haven't been challenged?
By keeping up with the work that designers and product managers are doing, a researcher can identify potential research questions based on the assumptions inherent within their decisions. Sometimes an external eye, like a researcher, can identify these when the decision maker themselves are unable to, so attending show and tells, and regularly keeping updated with the work of the teams, can help identify high priority research questions.

Is there enough time to run a study of appropriate quality?
As covered earlier, three weeks is an average amount of time that it may take to plan, run and debrief a study. Cutting that down will compromise the quality of the study, and the reliability or utility of the findings - care should be taken when considering committing to studies that do not allow the full process to be followed.

In addition to work for each product team, also explore whether there are any cross-team studies that would help promote the value of running research studies. This could include work to describe and define the audience of the company's products and sharing that with all of the product teams. By combining larger more strategic work with studies commissioned by product teams, it will help raise colleagues understanding of the types and value of research.

Over time, it is unsustainable to proactively source potential studies, and the dynamic should shift towards product teams coming forward with appropriate questions. Embedding researchers inside product teams is the most effective way of doing this, as is discussed later in this section. However, making sure teams are aware of the research studies that have occurred, and the value it has led to, is another avenue to help research studies emerge.

Some ways of achieving this include:
- Creating a dedicated slack channel which shares information from studies, including reports, videos, and steps teams have taken in reaction to the results of a study.
- Putting things on the wall that share the results from recent studies - for example the exec summary slides from each round of research, and any visual deliverables.
- Creating a team website which has links and information about the work that has been done.
- Sharing updates from studies at regular update meetings - e.g. weekly product team updates.
- Hosting open drop-ins where people can ask about research or studies that have occurred previously.
- Writing blog posts on a company blog.
- Hosting regular lunchtime sessions talking about research techniques or other aspects of the role that people show an interest in.

The goal of all of these is not necessarily to share the specific insights from these studies, but to create an understanding of how research studies have a history of creating relevant and useful information to make informed decisions for other people, which will encourage new people to commission research.

Throughout all these approaches, the framing should also make it clear how to book a research study, making the commitment as low as possible - e.g. starting with an informal chat with a member of the research team. Doing all of this will encourage people to think about incorporating research into how they work and will gradually improve the maturity of research inside the organisation.

Adding new methods

As discussed earlier in the book, the method used for research should be informed by the research questions the product team need answered. Early on in a team's maturity that is often usability testing, if the product exists already, or contextual research, if trying to learn about an audience to inform a product early in development. These methods are particularly good when working with teams who are new to research, because the output and benefit of them are immediately obvious, making research seem like a good return on investment. The approach we have covered for planning and running a study fits particularly well for interviews, observation, and usability testing, but eventually these will start to be limiting, and the team will want to add additional methods to answer new research questions that emerge.

Introducing new methods creates a reputational risk - when compared to the established methods that researchers are well versed in, there is an increased chance that the study will go wrong, requiring extra time to resolve or failing to appropriately answer all the research questions.

For this reason, it is sensible to pilot these studies extensively, and apply them in less visible settings first, before rolling it out to the most business-critical projects. This will prevent the messy introduction of a new method impacting people's perception of the quality of the wider research team's work and reduce the impact of other, robust, research studies.

Matching new methods and research questions

In part three of this book, we looked at how the appropriate method to use for a study is informed by the objectives, which is informed by 'what decisions do the team have to make next?'.

The methods discussed so-far focus on uncovering people's behaviour in the real world, to inform product decisions, and assessing their understanding and ability to use the things that have been made, to evaluate product decisions. However, there are other sorts of research questions, including:

- Do people like the thing we've made?
- How does people's behaviour or understanding change over time?
- How does people's behaviour with our product change based on where in the world they are?
- Can all the audience use this?

Some product team questions can't be reliably answered with the methods described previously, such as lab-based usability testing or contextual research based on seeing people do things in the real world, and other research methods are required. Methods that can be explored and added to the repertoire over time include opinion testing, diary studies, remote studies and accessibility testing, amongst others.

Opinion Tests

To reliably learn whether people 'like' the thing being tested, a combination of methods is required.
By gathering insights from a qualitative method such as interviews, a range of opinions about the thing being tested can be gathered. These interviews should be repeated until saturation is reached and every possible opinion has been captured.

These opinions can then inform a survey, where the representativeness of each opinion can be investigated - exploring what proportion of the audience agree with each opinion. This overcomes the challenge from interviews alone that it is unclear how prevalent each opinion is, leaving it difficult to draw conclusions about what to do.

This method needs care when being introduced, because surveys are subject to many biases, and it is not clear when those biases have impacted the results - such as people giving socially desirable answers rather than accurate ones. Careful wording of the questions and checking for consistency in what people have responded will help reduce this, but researchers should always be aware of the biases that are impacting the results they are getting, and the gap between reported behaviour and true behaviour.

Interpretation is also a challenge for the results from these studies. Asking for ratings is often common from teams, whether it is an overall score or using a measure like NPS. These are usually meaningless by themselves (what does it really mean for a feature that it has scored 6/10 rather than 7/10...), and only valuable when benchmarked against other things – however, even then there are risks that score differences are caused by the group being sampled changing, or the context in which the question was asked differing, rather than really representing a difference in the quality of the product.

Additionally, when communicating the results from these kinds of studies, the product team needs to understand that opinions do not necessarily correlate with achieving their business goals. There are plenty of products that people do not like, that are very successful - and on the other hand just because people like something doesn't mean they will use it - hence why behavioural studies are usually firmer ground to base business decisions on.

Despite all of these challenges, 'do people like the thing we're making, and why?' is a common research objective that a new team will be asked to tackle, and so introducing a robust and repeatable way of answering this will be to the long term benefit of the team, in combination with education about the risks of using this data to inform decision making.

Diary Studies

A limitation of running single-shot studies is that it is not possible to see how user's interactions change over time. When looking at prototypes in a lab, only their initial experience is captured - and although the initial interaction will have a huge impact on a user's experience with a product, it is not possible from that single study to anticipate how the issues will change over time - will people learn how to overcome problems? will their behaviour change? etc…

Learning how interactions change over time is often important - not just for testing products, but also to get a more realistic understanding of people's behaviour to inform product decisions, rather than relying on interviews and recollection to understand what participants do when not face to face with a researcher. For these types of research questions, adding the ability to run diary studies to a team can be valuable and increase the type of research objectives the team can reliably answer.

A diary study involves asking participants to capture their interactions or thoughts over time - e.g. filling out a daily log about what they have done, related to the topic of interest. For example, if working on a transport app, ask participants to log each time they use a mode of transport, because understanding this will inform product decisions. There will be some gaps when relying on user's recollection and dedication filling this out, and so supplementing self-reported information with automatic measures of what users are doing will increase the reliability of the information gathered.

A lo-fi way to start to trial this can be achieved with any survey tool, such as Google Forms, and creating some specific questions about people's behaviour related to the topic of interest can be sent to the participants daily as a way of capturing their behaviour over time. As with any survey questions, think about how the results will be analysed - a lot of large free-text boxes soon become a burden to analyse and interpret.

However, there are some constraints with using a survey tool that will require additional effort from a researcher to overcome, including remembering to send the surveys daily and chasing participants to complete it. Over time, moving to a dedicated diary study tool can add additional features - such as automatically reminding participants to fill out an entry, or allowing them to supply images or video, which will reduce the burden on the researcher running the study and increase the efficiency of the team. These tools often have a cost, so waiting until the demand for diary studies exists, due to the successful pilots with survey tools, will help avoid this being a wasted expense.

Remote studies

Another limitation that some of the methods previously covered have is that they only reach people who can be invited to come into the lab within a reasonable time. This creates the potential for sampling bias - people who live in remote locations (or just places far away from the research team) will not participate in research, and their behaviour or issues will be missed, without knowing if their behaviour is the same or different to closer participants.

To avoid this, adding the ability to perform remote research is sensible to allow the research team to evolve the services it offers. This involves using remote screen-sharing tools, such as Google Hangouts to be able to see and view the screen of participants without physically being in the same room and allows sessions to be run with participants from across the globe.

This method introduces many potential technical issues that will cause sessions to go wrong and is particularly important to trial in a safe setting before using it for a high-profile study. To help reduce the chance of problems occurring, testing the screen sharing software with participants before the session can help ensure they will be ready to go (and a participant recruiter can often help do this). Also running pilots to check the session runs as intended remotely is sensible, to avoid running into simple issues such as expecting participants to sign a consent form, without preparing a way of getting the form to them. Overbooking spare participants is also useful, because there will be an increased number of dropouts from remote studies, due to the low level of commitment required from participants, and technical complexity.

By printing off a map, and marking the areas participants come from, the team can track the areas that participants are based in, and spot areas that have been underrepresented. Combining lab research with remote research is one technique that can help reduce the risk of sampling bias occurring due to the method choices the team are making.

Accessibility

A critical, but often overlooked aspect of usability testing is evaluating accessibility. Some users require assistive technology or inclusively designed products in order to use them, due to temporary or permanent disabilities. A product that works for these audiences will benefit from both the opportunity to be used by a larger audience of people and reduce the risk of reputational damage occurring due to building exclusionary things.

It is perhaps incorrect to package this separately from other usability testing (why are issues caused by someone's previous experiences with software different to those caused by someone's disability?), but commonly done so, because recruitment of participants is more challenging for these audiences. As the research team grows, a sensible area to develop is addressing this oversight and ensuring that usability feedback is gathered from all the realistic audiences of the software.

Fundamentally, this is a participant recruitment issue, rather than introducing new methods, but accessibility research often falls into three groups:
- Automated Testing
- Expert Review
- Usability Testing

Automated Testing describes using online tools - such as Wave Web Accessibility Tool, to detect potential accessibility issues based on where the code is not compliant with best practice. This can help ensure a degree of compliance with accessibility standards but does not offer a complete evaluation of the product - many usability issues cannot be identified by automated tools, and passing the automated test won't give confidence that the product is 'accessible'. It can, however, be a first step of things to resolve before tackling a more extensive test.

Expert Accessibility Review is when a person or a group of people with experience with accessibility review the product and identify potential issues. This can often be performed by people who have the types of assistive technology needs that are being tested for such as screen-reader users. As with other forms of pseudo-test, there are limitations with this method, because the person performing the review will not be real users and will be unable to accurately reflect the context and behaviour of someone using the software for real. However, it will successfully identify more issues than automated testing, and can be easier to recruit than real users, because they are often run by professional organisations offering this service.

Usability Testing is always the most reliable way to identify the most prominent issues real users will have. However, recruitment becomes a real challenge, because the goal is to find real users who use the product, who also represent a comprehensive range of access needs. This pool of participants can be relatively small, depending on your product, and ensuring that a constant stream of new participants that meet this criterion is being uncovered is a beneficial area a participant recruiter could help with. Making a panel of users with access needs can help reduce the time for future recruiting for tests, but introduces the risk of re-using the same users, so needs to be done with care to prevent their experience from previous sessions biasing them for future sessions. Because of the challenges with recruiting, sometimes bad practise such as re-using users may have to be considered, but when done should be done knowingly, and the impact of doing so anticipated and mitigated.

Over time, improving a team's participant recruitment techniques so there is a supply of relevant users with access needs will make this process easier, and in the meantime supplementing gaps with automated testing and expert reviews will be better than not taking accessibility needs into account at all. Ensuring that products don't discriminate against people with disabilities is becoming an increasingly pertinent issue, backed up by legislation and public pressure, and being able to help with this is a valuable service for the research team to offer.

Piloting new methods

Each of these methods introduces technical complexity beyond basic usability testing and interviews, and so increase the opportunity for things to go wrong. As covered, piloting these methods on safe internal or low-profile projects before running them on business-critical projects can help reduce the chance for them to catastrophically fail and negatively impact people's opinion of the other work the team does.

Despite the risk, it is beneficial to ensure that the team is expanding its capability and is in a position where it has a range of methods to apply to answer research objectives robustly. Not only does introducing new methods introduce the opportunity for researchers to develop their own skills and demonstrate growth, but it also prevents the team getting stuck in the rut of being just a usability testing team, and creates the opportunity to influence decisions about what gets built, not just how things get built, increasing the impact of the research team.

Hiring and developing researchers

Early on, a lot of progress with advancing user research inside an organisation can be done with just one or two people. Researchers often works well in pairs - by having a second trained researcher taking notes from a research session, analysis time can be halved. However hopefully requests for research will grow over time, as successful projects start to increase awareness of the potential for user research throughout the development of products. This means that the team will have to grow, to keep up with demand.

Hiring for user researchers can be difficult. There are currently more companies that need user research than there are good researchers in the world, and so competition for good candidates is high. Finding good candidates will take a proactive approach and being where researchers are - such as attending or hosting industry events, using recruiters, or reaching out to personal contacts, in addition to longer term projects such as building the reputation of the company as a place where good research happens.

Assessing candidates

Having found potential candidates, assessing them often involves an interview, and a task - such as identifying some usability issues with a website and presenting them, to allow analytical and presentation skills to be assessed. During these assessments, some criteria that may be useful to identify good candidates include:

Understanding the design process
Regardless of any specific methodology, the candidate is able to describe how design works, and the process of identifying real problems in the world, exploring potential ways of resolving that problem, and assessing each potential solution for whether it solves the problem, makes money and avoids causing terrible things to happen to other people.

Understanding the role of user research

An awareness and ability to describe how user research both helps identify problems that exist in the world and inform potential solutions, as well as its role evaluating the things that are being built to see whether users understand and can use them.

Understanding the role of a user researcher

Being able to plan and run studies, while avoiding traps around giving their own opinions about issues instead of conclusions that can be backed up with robust data, and other things that may reduce the impartiality of research. However, also being prepared to being open to challenge dogma about how the role works - for example, regardless of whether they believe the role of researchers is to make recommendations or not, being able to describe both sides of the argument about why a researcher may or may not be the right person to make recommendations of what action to take based on the issues they learn in their studies. Other common sayings in UX, such as 'everyone is a designer', or 'quant tells you what, qual tells you why', are other areas where an understanding of both sides of a debate, and being able to give a justified opinion would indicate a good candidate.

Curiosity

Research (and 'UX' in general) is a field with many active debates, a lot of dogma, and a reasonable amount of nonsense mixed in. Being an active member of the community is a good indication that a researcher is dedicated to improvement, which can include listening to podcasts, viewing talks, joining slack communities, in addition to attending events. Many people have personal constraints on their time which can make attending events challenging, and so being broad in what is being looked for as evidence of curiosity about research is important to avoid excluding good candidates.

Attention to detail

A researcher's role is to give information to teams, and this requires a high degree of trust from product teams in the quality of the work of the research team. Once broken, trust can take a long time to rebuild, and one of the easiest ways of losing it is lacking attention to detail - for example, drawing over-reaching conclusions from a round of research, or just poor spelling reducing the level of credibility of a report. Looking for candidates who can demonstrate the appropriate level of care, and avoid sloppy mistakes, will help avoid risking the team's reputation. I recognise that this paragraph makes me a hostage to fortune for the rest of this book.

But also... none of the above. There is a huge risk when hiring to fall foul of subconscious biases, hiring people who look like the hiring manager's mental image of what a researcher looks like. The above factors to consider when hiring should not be taken as prescriptive, and be prepared to be open too, and be surprised by, candidates who don't fit these criteria.

Developing researchers

Hiring takes a lot of time and attention, and it is much cheaper and easier to keep a good researcher on the team than to find a new one. Offering growth opportunities at every level can help encourage people to stay, because they can see that their responsibilities will grow, and they will have the opportunity to add new skills. Precisely how this works will change in each organisation, but some of the distinctions between each level could include...

Junior Researcher
At this level, a new researcher will mostly assist on studies, and be given specific tasks to complete, such designing and analysing questionnaires, or preparing the materials for a study. After a period of exposure to working with more experienced researchers, they can start to take increased

responsibility for planning and delivering research, with less oversight, until they are ready to learn research by themselves.

Mid-Level Researcher
At this level, a researcher will be able to plan and execute upon well scoped study with minimal oversight. As they develop, they can start to proactively identify and scope appropriate research studies with teams, rather than having research projects scoped and handed over to them.

Senior Researcher
At this level, a researcher can be trusted to ensure that appropriate research is taking place by proactively identifying research opportunities and following through to ensure they happen, in addition to being confident and experienced at planning and delivering studies. They will need little oversight in order to plan and run studies. As they develop, they can demonstrate increased ownership over improving how the team works, including leading the introduction of new research methods to the team, or process optimisations.

Lead Research Practitioner
Above senior researcher, at many tech-lead companies, progression splits between practitioner and a management track. At this level, a practitioner will be confident with any sort of research study thrown at them, proactively ensuring that the right studies are happening for the products and are a reliable public face for the team, whether that is with internal clients or at external events.

Lead Research Manager
This role is at the same level as the lead research practitioner, but has a focus on management - e.g. line managing other researchers, creating opportunities to develop, as well as coordinating the overall work of the team - prioritising

projects and ensuring that an appropriate amount of research is happening in the right places.

Head of Research/Director of Research

This role sits at a senior level, and represents the discipline in strategic decision making at the top of the organisation. They can use that top-level access to advocate for and commission research studies to inform decisions at the most impactful time. A common challenge for organisations new to evidence-based decision making is not recognising the potential to run studies to inform product decisions before they are made, rather than just deciding how to implement them. At this level a researcher will be part of those conversations and can ensure that studies are run at the appropriate time to have an impact.

When the team is new is a great time to define how progression works, before people start to get itchy feet and think about moving on. Forming a new team is also a great time to give opportunities to demonstrate working at the level above, particularly through process projects, and work developing the team's process, while it's all still fresh and being defined. By showing other members of the research team clear opportunities for progression and making the tasks they could be doing to demonstrate progression explicit, it will help retain researchers and prevent re-hiring from being a distraction for the developing research team.

Making research collaborative

This book has described developing an internal research team in an 'agency' model, with a centralised user research group who are asked by product teams to do rounds of research for them. This is not the only way that researchers inside a company can function and may not be the most effective for identifying opportunities for research to occur or communicating the findings of research. However, it can be the most appropriate when the level of engagement from product teams is low - until product teams have been convinced of the benefits of developing a deep understanding of their users, their interest in research is largely in the results, not the details of how it was found or being involved in the process.

Over time, a research team should look at changing this and giving engaged product teams the opportunity to get closer to the process of running research, and researchers should be running research collaboratively with their product teams. There are some benefits of this approach, and some approaches that can be taken to achieve it.

Why run research collaboratively?

As the person designing, running, analysing, and communicating information about users, researchers often have the deepest level of understanding of them, their behaviour, motivations, and the opportunities to build suitable things for them. However, a researcher is not the person who makes decisions about what to do as a result of this information - they lack the same depth of contextual understanding about the goals of the product, or the expertise of other disciplines in interaction design, visual design or implementation to be able to do as good a job at deciding the right course of action as someone with different domain expertise.

This creates a communication gap between the people who understand users best, and the people who need to use that information to inform their decisions. Creating and presenting reports has some benefits for capturing the information in context and being suitable for sharing with a wider audience. However, they are not the only way to communicate what was learned, and some other methods may lead to a deeper understanding of users from the audience. This is what collaborative user research aims to achieve, by reducing the gap between 'learning about users' and the people who need to use that information.

Opening up research so a wider audience can play an active role in data collection, analysis, and documenting is not easy, and often particularly desired until teams have reached a certain level of research maturity, so is suitable as a longer-term project as the team grows. However, when implemented successfully it can lead to better decisions being made based on a deeper, truer, understanding of the needs of users. In this chapter, we'll look at a programme of collaborative activities for throughout the product development process.

Collaborating before running any research

As a first step with a new team, it is helpful to baseline everyone's assumptions and understanding about their users. This will not only help avoid running studies that repeat work previously done, but also highlight the assumptions and biases a team might have, which will influence how they receive any future findings. This will allow research findings to be positioned in an impactful manner.

One way of achieving this is starting a relationship with a new team with a proto-persona workshop. This is an interactive session where the team document their current understanding of the audience.

Proto-persona workshops are an established way of uncovering and documenting team's existing understanding of their audience for a project. However, the name 'proto-persona' can be quite technical and intimidating, and the word persona often comes with connotations - so consider using another name if it would help not scare people off.

To run this session requires:
- Some A3 paper
- Some post-its
- Some sharpies
- Some dot stickers if available
…As a person working in digital presumably these are always all close to hand!

Then find someone who knows why the company thinks a product should exist, such as the product manager or a senior stakeholder, and is happy to give a 5-minute recap to the team.

The actual session should be booked for 1.5 – 2 hours and can be split into different sections. After an introduction where a stakeholder or product manager reminds everyone what this project is, and the researcher recaps the goals of the workshop ('capturing what we already know, or think we know, about the users'), the activities begin:

Activity 1 – Listing all the potential audiences
First, ask everyone to list out all the potential 'types' of people that the team think might be the users for this project or product, and capture each one on post-it notes (one user type per post-it).
A common question from the group will be how granular the 'types of people' should be. The correct level of granularity is aiming to capture every type of person that we anticipate will have a significant behavioural difference from the other types of people listed.

This will take around 3-5 minutes, and by setting everyone the goal of coming up with at least four types of users, we should end up with plenty of raw material.

After this, everyone on the team should have a pile of post-its, with types of users written on them.

Activity 2 – Theming and prioritising users
Now we want to recognise the duplication within the 'types' of users identified, and pick which ones the product team want to focus on. To help manage this, it can often be useful to have two axes to plot all of the users on. The axis will depend on the subject matter the product is focused around but can include things like:
- expert vs non-expert
- time sensitive vs not-urgent
- nearby vs geographically remote
- high impact vs low impact

Pick two, or come up with others based on the subject being looked at...

Mark the two axes on the wall, like these examples for coffee shop users:

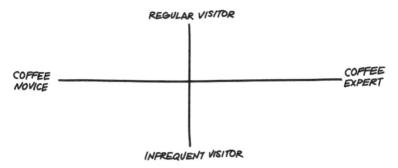

Decide on two axes and mark them on the wall

Then in turn have everyone read out their post-its and decide where they go on the axis. After each one is read out, ask if anyone has the same type of user, or one very similar, and stick them together. Go around everyone, until all of the audience types have been covered and stuck on the wall.

At this point, consider creating group names to represent batches of similar post-its. For example, if there are post-its representing 'students', 'high school kids', 'home school kids', 'school-goers', this might be grouped under the same heading for the time being of 'students', because they are similar audiences (at least, that's our assumption before running some real research).

This exercise may have ended up with a lot of different audiences – too many to handle in one session. The next task is to prioritise which to focus on in the final bit of this workshop, which will guide early research efforts. To do this, assign every team member three votes, and ask everyone to vote for the audience that they think is a priority to focus on currently. Voting can either be done by sticking 'dot' stickers on the post-its or marking with a sharpie if the team doesn't have dot-stickers.

Depending on the team, sometimes it can be sensible to give project owner, or other important stakeholders, more stickers in the vote.

After voting, hopefully some of the groups would have emerged as a priority to focus on – ideally 3-4 types of users. Now onto the third activity.

Activity 3 – Capturing what we already know about them
Having selected the most important types of user to focus on first, the last part of the workshop focuses on capturing what the group already know, or think they know, about these people. To do this, ask everyone to split into groups – one group per 'type' of priority user.

Give each group a type of user, and a big sheet of paper, and ask them to split it into four sections. Then title each section – 'Goals', 'Needs', 'Pain-points', and space for a picture.

PICTURE:	GOALS:
NEEDS:	PAIN POINTS:

Split the paper into four areas

Explain to the groups what each of these sections are:
- In 'Goals', ask them to capture what this audience is trying to get done (in regards to the subject being looked at) – for example, if defining the audience for a coffee shop, a goal might be to 'get a hot drink on my way to work'.
- In 'Meeting their needs', ask the group to capture what we would need to provide to allow these users to meet their goals – e.g. for the coffee shop example the needs may include "be able to take the drink away with me", "get my drink promptly so I can get to work on time", "my drink is still warm when I get to work". All of these will be great things to research to understand in greater depth.
- In 'Pain-points' the groups should describe what they assume is difficult for these people currently. For example, "I can't see what drinks are available

until I'm at the front of the queue", "People making big orders slow down me getting my drink", etc.

Give every group 10-15 minutes to fill out their paper, and then ask each group to play it back to everyone else. During the play-back, ask the wider group to comment, in order to capture anything that might have been missed, or anything that the group feel is suspect. These are good areas to highlight for future research to explore and validate.

Once everyone is done, take away the paper that people have made, and stick them on the wall. This can be the basis for the team's future research.

A filled in proto-persona

When working with teams that are new to research, they may think that because this session is being run by a user researcher, that it is "doing user research". It is not – no-one has spoken to any users, and no (primary) research has occurred. It is important to frame the workshop correctly with teams so that they understand and recognise this, as part of the wider education about the role of research, and so that they do not confuse the reliability and 'true-ness' of their assumptions, with the reliability of the findings from rigorous user research. Despite that, the benefits of running this workshop to focus team members on their users, and for uncovering their current level of understanding make this activity worth running to inform future studies.

Planning a study collaboratively

The ethos of running research collaboratively is opening each stage of the research process up so that non-researchers can play a meaningful role in it, better understand the findings and become more invested in the outcome of research. There are many ways in which this could be achieved, depending on the stage of a round of research.

As covered previously, research objectives are 'what you're going to learn from research', not the actual questions that would be asked to a user directly in an interview and getting consensus on them should be the first step when planning any study. Failing to agree on the research objectives will lead to disagreements later on about the appropriate method and the actual questions that will be asked to users– so it is important to do this collaboratively and involve all the decision makers for the project.

As covered in part three of this book, this can be run as a workshop that asks the product team to identify and prioritise what to work on.

If the work on proto-personas described previously has been done before planning studies, that can also inspire some questions ("do people really have these problems?", "have we missed other problems they have currently?", "are the behaviours between these two types of people real?"). Research objectives will typically fall into some broad categories of:
- What are people trying to do currently, related to the domain our topic is in?
- How do they do it currently?

- Why do they do it in that way?
- What's difficult for them currently?
- What's confusing about doing it currently?

After, ask the product team to generate post-it notes of their research questions for discovery. The team should then prioritise them to identify "what are the most important ones for the team to understand first?" Dot voting, as we saw in the proto-persona workshop, is one way of doing this in a collaborative manner. This will give the researcher a prioritised list of the things that the team feel they need to learn during discovery, and will inspire the research run throughout this period (regular re-prioritisation with the product team will also be useful).

Running a study collaboratively

As previously covered, there is a lot of preparation before a study can commence, and the wider team should be involved with defining what that study will learn and be exposed to the process of preparing a study. There are further opportunities to make the study open and collaborative when actually running the research. The user researcher will likely be most experienced in good interview technique, and appropriate approaches for observing participants perform contextual tasks. However, as a collaborative team member, the goal of the researcher is not just to run good research, but to expose the rest of the team to it. That can include:
- Livestreaming the study, and allowing others to follow along
- Bringing team members along to the session, and asking them to take notes or transcribe
- Allowing team members to follow a scripted guide and speak to users themselves

The 'best' activity depends on several factors, including how engaged the team are, their maturity with research, and the logistics of this specific round of research.

As the team's engagement and interest rises, new collaborative activities become appropriate

Allowing teams to watch research

This is the lowest level of engagement that a team can achieve, but is not necessarily an easy sell for a disengaged team. The technical setup for live streaming an interview, or observing what a user is doing on a computer can be relatively easy to achieve, using the tools covered in part two of this book. By streaming the session to another room, the researcher is creating the opportunity for teams to observe the sessions live and take some meaning from them. This has some benefits but is not without its risks.

Some benefits of live observation
- Teams can see what happens in a research session first-hand and get a deeper understanding of the process.
- Teams become more familiar with their users, and their faith in the representativeness of any research findings is increased.
- Watching a session doesn't feel like a big commitment and is the least intimidating way for a non-researcher to get involved in the process.

Some risks with live observation
- Teams will get bored watching the session, stop paying attention, and look at their phones instead.

- Teams can find it difficult to make time for the sessions, and do not consider it a priority for their job.
- The researcher has no oversight of what conclusions the viewers are drawing from the session, and the team could go away and act based on an incomplete understanding of the findings.

So, what can be done to minimise these risks? How about increasing the commitment to collaboration...?

Asking a team to take notes
Teams will be more engaged if they are given something to do, and taking notes is a useful thing they can do. The easiest to understand, but most frustrating way of taking notes is transcribing - writing a verbatim record of everything the participant says and does. That's helpful for reference but can often be a difficult job (it requires a lot of fast typing) that is of low value if the transcript is not used as part of the analysis process.

Much more helpfully, the product team could be taking notes of only the significant parts of the study such as key quotes from the users or noting actions users took that seem particularly significant or relevant. With a mature team, this can helpfully remove a job that the researcher would otherwise have to do later. But it can be challenging to recognise what is worth capturing and relies on a degree of research maturity that takes time to work up too. Collaborative pre-study work, as described earlier, such as generating the research questions together and going through the study plan as a group before the sessions can help raise the team's ability to recognise good or useful things to note.

Benefits of team-notetaking
- It can reduce the amount of work a researcher needs to do to capture notes from the sessions.

- It gives raw ingredients that can enable further collaborative activities, like group analysis (covered later).

Risks of team notetaking
- Poor notes can fail to capture the right information, and researchers will want to be confident that everything relevant has been noticed. This can mean taking more time for reviewing the recording and writing additional notes.
- To get good quality notes requires the team to have the free time and interest to be committed to doing the pre-work.

It can be really helpful to give teams guidance on good notes, to help improve the quality of what they're capturing.

Good note taking guidance for teams

Some characteristics of good notes, to share with the product team before they are asked to do note-taking

Capture what happened or what was said, not an interpretation of what that means

Capture when and where the issue occurred, and which participant encountered it

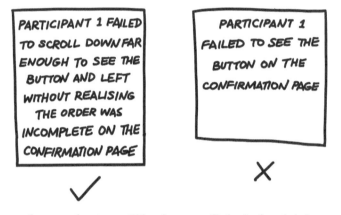

Capture the complete issue. What happened? And what did that cause to occur?

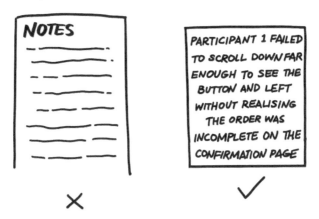

Capture the notes in the right format. For some analysis techniques, this might be post-its. For other teams, an excel spreadsheet or a mind-map might be appropriate.

Allowing teams to moderate the session
After a team member has been exposed to research for a while, they may feel brave enough to interview users themselves. This shows a high level of commitment and is a great step forward for team members - a positive sign that they value understanding users to inform decision making.

For the researcher, this means a change to the focus of their role on the team from individual contributor to facilitator. Coaching the team through running the interviews, giving feedback on how the questions were asked, and having oversight of the notes captured all become the most impactful part of the role. It also gives the researcher freedom to own the note-taking process and ensure that the notes captured are relevant and reliable, screening out any data that has been compromised due to poor questioning technique.

Benefits of team members moderating
- It exposes the team directly to their users, creating the opportunity for them to understand their users at a deeper level.

- It gives the researcher the opportunity to do other roles during the session, such as taking excellent notes.

Risks of team members moderating
- As new interviewers, teams may ask bad questions, either leading the participant or failing to probe appropriately to uncover information in appropriate depth to act. It will take time and practise before the maximum value is extracted from each session.
- Interacting with users directly requires the product team members to step outside of their comfort zone, and so requires a level of research maturity that can take a while to reach.

As the person in charge of the study, the researcher should be responsible for capturing the appropriate notes from the session, which will help minimise the impact of bad questions. Giving feedback on the interview technique, will also help improve this over time also.

Analysing a study collaboratively

Regardless of the collaborative approach taken in the study, the objective of each of these methods is to expose the product team to the raw experience of users, rather than interpreted findings. This has some risks, such as teams jumping to conclusions early, that will have to be managed by explaining the research process. However, it also creates the potential for better work to occur - the product team will know their discipline's specialism in more depth than a researcher would, and will be able to spot and interpret the cause of issues, or the gap between the experience the user had and the designed experience with a deeper level of subject matter expertise than a researcher working alone would.

There is a time between 'collecting data' and 'sharing findings' where the researcher normally has to go away and think about what the data shows.

This synthesis process is where their expertise as a user centred person, and understanding of the needs of the team are very valuable in distilling the raw information into clear 'bits' of information that will inform the team's understanding of their users, and impact the work they do. Opening up the early part of this analysis and synthesis process to the wider team is challenging, but is also another opportunity to benefit from their domain knowledge, and exposes them to 'raw' information, building up their understanding of their users and increasing the chance that product decisions will be informed by a real understanding of their user's context.

To run analysis collaboratively, there needs to be some raw material. This can be

- The transcripts of what was said in the interview.
- The product team's own notes of what they saw or heard in the sessions.
- The researcher's prepared notes based on what happened in the sessions.

With any of these kinds of raw notes, there is the opportunity to run a collaborative analysis session.

Running a collaborative analysis session
The goal of this session is to take all the information that everyone in the team has captured and draw some meaning from it - with enough fidelity that the team can act based on it.

This requires a room with lots of wall space - and some post-its, blue tack and the largest pieces of paper that can be found. The session can take up to two-hours.

Getting concepts down

The raw data captured from the research could potentially be in a lot of different formats - handwritten notes, typed transcriptions, or annotations on a video or image. The first step is to standardise how they are captured, and post-its are a great way of doing this. Ask all attendees to write up their raw notes onto post-its, following the 'good notes guidance' advice above of one concept per post-it. Many people will forget to prepare the post-its in advance - be prepared to dedicate the first 15-minutes of the session to writing the post-its.

Preparing the space

This session involves sticking the post-its up on the wall and finding the meaning within them. It helps to section the room into different topics, in order to place post-its on similar concepts close to one another. To achieve that, put some headings up around the room - starting with ones to represent the research objectives that the study was designed to answer, but with some blank to fill in when other themes emerge.

If the product team do not have permanent use of the room, stick up big sheets of paper for the post-its to go on (rather than going on the wall directly), so that they can be taken away after for more in-depth analysis.

When the team have their notes captured on post-its and the headings are stuck up, it is time to dive in.

Sharing with the team

In turn, each member of the team should read out their post-its to the room. After reading it out, they should decide against which heading to stick it, or whether a new heading is required.

The researcher who is facilitating the session may notice some concepts come up multiple times - for example, because multiple users said it, or due to corresponding information coming up from different data sources. When that occurs, stick them next to each-other.

Collaborative analysis in progress

After the first team member has read out their notes, the next person gets started, until the wall is covered in post-its.

Theming
The group then should theme the notes - find post-its that are talking about the same point and put them together. This activity works well in pairs, each looking at a section of the wall. When the pair have a theme, write a header on a post-it of a different colour explaining what the theme of the post-its within it are. After 20 minutes, each pair can share their themes with the room.

Taking it away
After all the themes have been discussed, it is important to explain to the team that this is not the end. The analysis that has occurred in this group session has been very shallow - one of the main benefits has been getting people to look at the data and think about it, rather than leading to any deep

insights immediately. Make sure to set expectations that the researcher will take it away and come back with a more thorough analysis.

Having completed a collaborative analysis session, the researcher has been given a structure for some of the findings that should be explored in more depth, and the team will have had some steer in their thinking. But there is still a lot of work to do - the product team will have only skimmed the surface of these topics, and there is a lot of relevant information from the study that would have been missed. That is why the output of collaborative analysis is not enough by itself to capture the appropriate depth of information that will have been uncovered in a good study and a researcher will still have to go away and think about it more.

This would typically involve the researcher taking time to review the recording of the session, and any transcripts or notes that have been captured. The researcher will be looking to find explanations - why do things occur? What is the impact of them? and spend time thinking about and articulating all the things that the study uncovered.

Debriefing a study collaboratively

After the in-depth analysis has been completed, it is time to present it back to the team. When presenting findings back to a team, this is also an opportunity to encourage active engagement with the results from the study, and help the team take that forward into actions. In the debrief section in part three of this book, we covered running debrief workshops as an alternative to giving recommendations where the wider team collaboratively suggest ways to address the issues. Facilitating this kind of workshop after presenting results can help teams think about the practical implications of the research findings on a deeper level, and actually do something off the back of research.

The risks with collaborative research

As an organisation's maturity with user research increases, opening up the research process to encourage active involvement from a wider group of people can be very beneficial - reducing the time required for studies to start informing decisions, removing the communication gap between researchers and decision makers and increasing everyone's understanding of their users to help them make sensible decisions.

However, it can have the potential to go wrong, including:
- Product team members acting prematurely without seeing the study to completion
- Product team members making decisions based on unsafe conclusions
- Useful information being missed by inexperienced team members
- People unrelated to the team viewing parts of the study, and drawing incorrect conclusions about what user research is

Allowing any of these risks to occur will reduce the quality of the output of research sessions, negatively influencing people's perceptions of the work of the research team and reducing the impact that the research team's studies have. This is a bad thing and to be avoided, which requires vigilance.

One aspect to think about when managing the risk of collaborative research is the relationship between collaboration and accuracy and drawing an appropriate balance. Assuming that a trained researcher will always do a better job at the design, execution and analysis of a study, but that the rest of the team are able to understand and apply the findings better the more involved they are, any study can be plotted on a scale, like this:

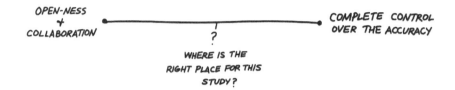

Collaboration and control need to be balanced, and studies planned appropriately.

Consciously thinking about the correct position on this scale for each study, based on the research maturity of the team, the priority of the study, and the consequences for either bad communication or bad work will allow the research team to make informed decisions about how collaborative each study should be. Over time this becomes easier, as the product team's understanding and ability to perform research related tasks improve, they no longer become conflicting principles.

When opening up the work of creating, running, and analysing studies to become a collaborative process across the whole product team, some steps can be taken to improve the accuracy of non-researcher's work. Regular guidance activities facilitated by the researcher will help everyone in the team do a better job at research tasks - for example, briefing them just before the sessions to cover what the research objectives are, how the tasks answer the objectives, and what to be looking out for. Recapping these before the analysis will also help improve the quality of the conclusions being drawn, in addition to reviewing any conclusions, before they are shared wider and used to inform decisions.

Taking responsibility for the quality of all research work, not just that run by researchers, is particularly important when organisations look to scale research. This can occur when organisations want to address the problem of having less researchers than required cheaply, by asking product teams to run their own research. The quality of research run by non-researchers can often be low, and errors such as relying too heavily on surveys, unmoderated methods and self-reported data can lead to poor quality insights being drawn. This will have a significant impact on people's perception of the value of user research, making it harder for robust, high-quality research to cut through the noise.

Firmness is important to manage this, establishing clear criteria for what is good or bad user research, and assessing other teams work against this. Some sensible review points can include:
- Reviewing the proposed study after a kick-off to ensure that the proposed research objectives can be answered by the intended research method.
- Reviewing the study design when written to ensure it will address the research objectives appropriately.
- Reviewing the findings from a round of research before they get debriefed to a team, to ensure that the conclusions stand up against the evidence.

After the video game crash of 1983, in which poor quality games were one of the causes, Nintendo launched their seal of quality - a logo on each game published officially on their console, to indicate that they believed this was a high-quality product and approved of it. A similar branding exercise, where work done by other teams can be approved by the 'official' user research team, is a tool that can be used to create an incentive to engage with the user research team and increase the quality of the research they are running.

Making reviews from the research team part of the process for how research works, and openly sharing the research process guidelines and templates across the organisation can help set expectations of what good research is, and give researchers the opportunity to catch bad work before it impacts people's perceptions of user research.

Building a research repository

Over time, user researchers learn a lot of useful information about their users, often for different product teams - and that information may be relevant and useful for other groups beyond the product team who commissioned the study. This creates the opportunity to find ways to share information learned from research across teams and avoid teams repeating studies that have already occurred or failing to review all the relevant information available to inform their decisions.

Depending on the likelihood that findings will be relevant and useful across teams, there are a few approaches that can be taken, each requiring a different level of effort. The least intrusive way of doing this is ensuring that proper documentation occurs around each study, and that it is clear where to find the objectives and findings from previous studies. Some techniques for doing this previously covered include having an internal team website, supported by real-world signposting from posters, indicating what studies have been run, what they learned, and where to find this. Incorporating the best practise from the debriefing section in part three of this book will make this not overly difficult to achieve and will allow other teams to self-serve and discover findings relevant to their work.

However, this method does associate the research findings to a specific round of research. Removing findings from being tied to a specific round of research can sometimes be beneficial, because it allows new queries to be run against them and patterns to emerge across rounds of research.

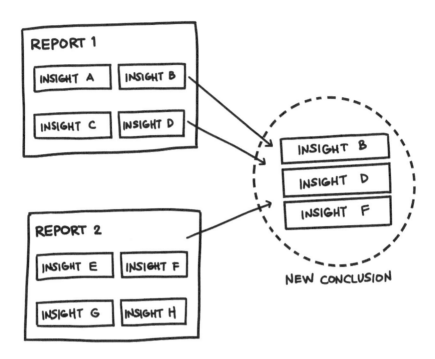

Freeing findings from studies can lead to new conclusions being discovered.

This requires creating a research repository, and doing some additional work at the end of each round of research:
- Taking the findings from that round of research
- Tagging them appropriately
- Adding them to the place where findings go

Each of these will be covered in turn.

To extract the findings requires looking through what was learned in a study and pulling out each discrete piece of information. For usability testing captured in the format documented earlier, a finding would be a slide, including the cause and impact - for example *"The back button was missed - cause: the back button was located in a non-standard place, and had low contrast- impact: users failed to identify how to go back, and cancelled the transaction when trying to make changes to previous pages. This greatly increased the amount of time they needed to complete the transaction*". For discovery research, focused on understanding an audience, this will include the thing learned, and why that is the case, for example, "*Car buyers consider price to be one of the main factors influencing their decision. Many car buyers have a specific budget allocated to their purchase, and so finding ones in the appropriate price range was more important than the other factors such as safety or mileage*". One round of research will have many findings, typically the contents of what was presented in the debrief and listing all of these out is the first step.

Tagging the findings can be difficult - tags will be one of the key ways future people will discover the findings again, and so it requires a good understanding of what criteria people will be using to explore previous findings. One important thing to tag for each finding is the round of research in which it was discovered, which allows traceability if a future user wanted to check the provenance of that finding. However, some other useful criteria for tagging can include the 'type' of user the finding relates to, the subject matter that is covered in the finding, and the level of confidence in the finding. Over time, these tags will evolve as the types of queries that people want to make against previous findings becomes clearer - taxonomies are hard, and an internal research study on the needs of people for accessing this data, which will inform new tags would make a suitable team task.

Deciding the type of repository to store all these findings in also depends on the needs of the team. Early on a spreadsheet, with fields for the finding, round of research and tags could be enough to achieve the goals of making previous findings discoverable and queryable. Air table is particularly useful for this by allowing references to other tables or fields within a field - making complex queries easy to achieve. Over time, the parts of this repository can be decoupled - inputting findings can be automated via scripts to be extracted from reports instantly and tagged appropriately. A database can hold the findings, and a more mature interface for querying the database could allow more complex queries. Again, the process of upgrading and iterating how research findings are shared requires a good understanding of the needs of those querying the findings and is a suitable topic for team tasks.

Creating a place to keep previous research findings can be a valuable tool for exposing previous findings, preventing redoing work and allows new conclusions to be drawn. It can also be particularly useful for teams that do have a continuous flow of new data without the time to explore it appropriately - for example, teams who have ended up in a situation where they run regular user interviews or surveys as benchmarking exercises, without explicit research objectives for each round. By putting the findings from those benchmarking exercises in a queryable format, then they can be useful data to explore when answering future research objectives that emerge in more well-defined studies.

However, there are also some risks to be aware of when creating a research repository. There is a time cost when creating and maintaining a database of previous findings, and a new research team need to be sure it is creating value for them to make that time commitment worthwhile. In addition, although removing findings from the 'wrapper' of being associated with a study does make them queryable, it does lose the context of the study that uncovered this finding. That greatly increases the chance that the finding may be misinterpreted or applied to situations where the findings are not relevant, creating unreliable information for decisions, which will impact on people's perceptions of the quality and reliability of all findings from the research team. A repository is particularly vulnerable to people exploiting it to find data to support preconceived conclusions, the opposite of what user research should be doing. For this reason, tight control and oversight over who is accessing the research repository, and what they are doing with the information acquired from it is important to ensure that the repository does not end up becoming a weapon for internal politics.

Part 5:

The end

Building User Research Teams

Having got this far, a new research team has started to educate the organisation about the benefits of building products with a user centred approach, established its processes and the ability to run tests, and successfully ran some studies that have provided valuable information to inform business decisions. Everyone at the organisation is happier, more well informed, and placing orders for their new yachts because of all the successful products that have been made.

We have also covered some areas in which a new research team can develop and improve over time, to set it on a path of increasing its capability and growth.

Of course, this all sounds easy when written down, however, in the real world, there will be many more challenges to overcome, and it can be incredibly difficult and demoralising. Some of those challenges can include:

- Disagreements with senior staff who feel challenged by information that conflicts with their existing preconceptions
- A lack of appropriate budget or time given to run high quality research
- Disinterest in the outcome of research, and studies failing to have an impact that they deserve

Despite these setbacks, decisions are still being made about products every day, and research can still help improve the quality of those decisions. The techniques we have covered will address these challenges over time. Optimism, and a sustained enthusiasm for pushing the cause of making decisions based on better quality information is therefore very important for new research teams. As user researchers, we are confident that we can bring value into decision making and are competent enough that we can identify the right opportunities and run high quality studies that will help everyone make better decisions. Because of this, the job of talking about and promoting a user centred mindset is just as important as being able to run good studies and will be where a lot of a new research team's attention is focused, supported by a cadence of regular studies.

Good luck!

Templates

Earlier chapters described how to create some of the templates that a new team should need, which will help disseminate best practice across researchers, and reduce the time each individual study needs to run. This included:

- A research project tracker
- The kick-off document
- The study plan/discussion guide
- The consent form
- The participant information sheet
- Information for security
- Viewing information for observers
- A note-taking template
- A debrief template

Many of these templates will be unique to each individual organisation and context, and so requires individual attention. However to get you started I have produced some guide templates that can be adapted for your own team. These are available on the website www.buildinguserresearchteams.com alongside other updates on how to continue to embed new user research teams.

Further reading

There are many great books about user research - some of which I feel are particularly helpful for a new research team. If budget allows, consider starting a research library to allow all the team to share books!

Just Enough Research by **Erika Hall**
This book is a great introduction to running research using a variety of methods, and some artefacts that can be created to communicate research findings. It promotes an enthusiasm for research, and deals with many real-world scenarios that researchers will have to address. As such, it's a great book to share with other researchers as they join the team, to help instil a shared understanding and ethos about how research works and how it fits into the design process.

Games User Research by **Anders Drachen, Pejman Mirza-Babaei** and **Lennart Nacke**
This book focuses on how user research applies to the development of video games. Despite being a games book, many of the principles are applicable to researchers in other contexts. In particular, David Tisserand's chapter on articulating and iterating upon the research process has been a big inspiration for me personally when developing semi-structured research processes in other organisations. There are other great chapters on research methods, and on the development of a usability lab, that can be relevant to researchers anywhere.

Don't Make Me Think and **Rocket Surgery Made Easy** by **Steve Krug**
Don't Make Me Think is an introduction to the concepts behind usability testing, aimed at a non-researcher audience. It is intended to be the right length to read during a plane ride, and so is suitable for sharing with anyone inside an organisation who is interested in learning the basics of what

usability testing is, as a gateway to other more varied research studies. Rocket Surgery Made Easy is a guide to planning and running usability studies and may be suitable for teams who are interested in research but can't be supported by the new research team until the team has scaled up, as a way of managing demand.

Quantifying the User Experience by **Jeff Sauro** and **James Lewis**
Accuracy, particularly when working with colleagues who have a strong statistical background, is very important for building credibility. This book is a practical guide to applied statistics for user research and is invaluable when dealing with surveys or other quantitative data.

Another invaluable support mechanism is the wider research community. Researchers are often a very friendly and inclusive bunch, and there are plenty of meetups and community forums that give researchers the opportunity to ask for guidance, share techniques and best practise, or find a shoulder to cry on. Active participation in the research community has lots of benefits, such as exposing teams to new ideas or approaches, helping find good candidates for research roles and providing recommendations on vendors or software. Seeking out these groups can be a fantastic support network and will improve the growth and emotional health of a research team.

Acknowledgements

This book is inspired by lessons I've learned from all the lovely researchers I have worked with before, and many of them will recognise things we've discussed, things they have taught me, or mistakes we've made together, as the inspiration for the preceding chapters.

I will not list everyone individually, for fear of leaving people out, but if you think you recognise a conversation we have had in this book, you are probably right, and I'm grateful for what it taught me. Thanks to all the amazing researchers I worked with at PlayStation, for teaching me how user research should work, and to all the user centred design team at Parliament for teaching me there were other ways a research team could function, as well as the Games User Research community for their continued guidance and wisdom.

Special thanks to my wife Emma for all her support in the creation of this book.

Thanks also for reading this book. If you are feeling kind, please leave a review on amazon - I am told they are important!

About the author

Steve Bromley is a London-based user researcher, with ten years of experience running research with companies such as American Express, PlayStation, Parliament and at the UK's largest commercial publisher. He has given guest lectures at the University of Sussex and the University of Ontario Institute of Technology, has presented at conferences including GamesUR, The Research Thing, UXBrighton and CHIPlay, and his work has featured at GDC and at the Develop conference.

This experience has taught him a bit about building research teams, which he is enthusiastic about sharing!

He has previously written the chapter on Interviewing Players for the Games User Research book, and a chapter on Measuring Social Interaction for the Multiplayer: Social Aspects of Digital Gaming book.

He has a personal blog covering user research for games and software, which is at www.stevebromley.com

In 2021, Steve released another book about user research – covering how to get a job as a user researcher for video games and how to run great playtests. Find more at www.gamesuserresearch.com

Made in United States
Troutdale, OR
06/30/2023

10905039R00126